You Were Built to Create Cool S**t

A friendly guide to exploring your curiosity and crafting a better world

Copyright © 2023 by jack friks

All rights reserved.

Table of Contents

Preface
Introduction 1
You were built to create (cool sh*t) 10
You + Creation 17
Creation is in everything 26
A lesson from my grandpa on creation 29
Creativity over IQ 34
Craftsmanship 39
Consumption decay 44
Focus on what you want 52
Explore your curiosity 55
Becoming a graceful idiot 62
Just get started 66
Creation is innate 71
Being a purple cow 74
Creation as a superpower 75
Creation vs progress 77
You have enough time. 84
The real creators (you) 87
The usefulness of chance 89
Starting over 92
Everyone is winging it 95
Play comes before work? 98
Create every single day 103
Trying more stuff 105

Something I wish someone would have told me
earlier but I'm kinda glad they didn't 109

A friendly pep talk..112

Learning without pressure to perform and
the ghost of dread..116

Information overload..120

The rules are made up and no one cares 124

The Creation Megaphone 129

Time in *the zone,* and *going deep* 133

Boredom is a gift... a good gift..136

Your animal spirit (life as a movie) 140

Lacking inspiration?..144

The right way, or the wrong way, or your way? 147

My vision of creation, for reference 153

The Do 100 approach...158

Growing up... it's not worth it?..166

Have you tried just having fun? 171

Effortless creation? Lightweight Curiosity? 176

The purpose of beauty and it's creations 179

Giving light to the grim reaper..180

Creating stuff to find thyself..183

Creating for money...188

Finding your own approach 198

Disregarding parts of your instincts 199

Thinking too much and creating nothing...................... 202

Curiosity as a benchmark for success 207

Agency: figure it out, yourself!	211
Creating your own home	215
The undercover creation agent	219
Waves of joy in all the crevasses	224
Letting people convince you that something is wrong with you	229
Making the internet a better place	233
Creating the conclusion	238
Free resources	241
Reading List	243

(•‿•) /

A tiny nudge of encouragement costs nothing, but it has made **all the difference** in my life. *So...*

To my mom, my dad, my future wife, my friends, and my past self: thank you for encouraging me and thank you for believing in me, even when it probably didn't make sense to do so.

\ (˘‿˘)

Preface

This book is not a prescription to all of your problems (sorry my friend).

Instead, this book is here to show you a collection of thoughts about creation, and curiosity; all of which are aimed to help you create some cool sh*t and make some meaningful noise so you can craft a better world beneath your own two feet.

If you have any opposition to my words, then good! It's this book's job to help you find where your own ground lies – Put to use what you find useful, discard the excess: I will not be offended in any way.

If you can: think of me as your encouraging spirit, like a friend cheering you on. Just like a faithful friend, this book is not going anywhere. So, if at any point while reading this book you feel inspired to create, or to act: then go do so. Put this book down immediately.

Regardless of having me as your encouraging spirit, the journey will be long. You can always rest in the pages of this book, but only if you promise to get back out there to continue on your path of creating your own cool sh*t. The game of creating things is your entire life, it always has been. Now that you are aware of this game...

It's time to become a key player in your own existence. It's time to create some cool sh*t.

Introduction

A little while back in the time of cavemen and cavewoman, humans smashed rocks against rocks to showcase their brain power. Now (some years later), here we are—here you are—existing today in a wonderous world full of creation.

For a second, let's imagine that you weren't here today but instead you were born two-point-five *million* years ago. As you wake up on the cold, hard, dirt ground you sense something happening near your feet. Is it a lion? Is it your tribe leader coming to bonk you over the head with a rock? Is it rainwater seeping closer to your naked body? Well, I can tell you one thing: it's certainly not a sunny side up breakfast in bed. In this reality, you wouldn't be hoping for bacon and eggs, or pancakes, rather you'd be hoping for anything, as long as it's not nothing.

Today things are much different. You can pull out your phone, click four buttons, and your food is on its way to your doorstep. You don't have to talk to another human or walk more than 30 steps. Your delivery driver is less than an hour away at any time, completely at your disposal.

How did we get here? Well, all of this came from someone somewhere using their creation abilities. Time crawled and along the line of time improvements were made, things were created, we continued on this path, and that's how we got to where we are today: to a world where **you** can create in abundance, where the possibilities are only expanding.

Although what we have today is advanced in comparison to two million years ago, let's be honest: you don't have to go back a million years to view today as advanced. The things we create on a daily basis today would have been thought of as witchcraft just in the prior century alone. Yet living today, with the world containing more creations than ever before, many humans are still afraid to create things, to even try. Why is this?

Because humans are distracted and stuck. Stuck in consuming more than they create. Not just sometimes, but all the time. Without acknowledging how things are, how can we ever hope to change them for the better? How can we as humans harness our creative powers and, create some more cool s**t?

Now, you may be thinking something along the lines of "I can't create stuff; I'm not the creative type" or another lie in a similar fashion. Self deceit will do you little good. If you really think about it, deep down you know that you can create things, you know you have creative ability, and you know you've been denying yourself from using such abilities for far too long. Creating things is very simple: To bring something into being. Gardening for creating crops, cooking for creating a meal, calling your mom for creating a connection, painting for creating art, management for creating order, creating love in a family or a relationship, creating questions to move yourself forward. Creation is framed, and deeply imbued in everything we do. Another thing about creation is that it mustn't always be an artform, but all creations have a form of artistry inside them. You are the artist of your world.

Everyday people just like you have been creating things for centuries, millennia even.

A guy down the street (from someone) invented the basics of rocket propulsion and space travel. Someone's best friend created the internet. A random kid grew up and then created the iPhone. Your mom created you – need I give any better examples of creation? The list goes on and by the end of this book, you'll know better how you're an important part of it too.

Here we are: it's astonishing to even exist, never mind at this point in time: when creation is at its peak. We've never known more than we know now as humans and the reason anything is anything is because someone somewhere used their given creation abilities to make it so.

You may remember a feeling of true wonder and creation as a kid, but after a certain point in adolescence most of us seem to leave our key creation senses behind: our senses of wonder, curiosity, imagination... are all often flushed away by the idea that we should "grow up" and stop dreaming: "get your head out of the clouds jimmy!".

These elements are crucial for creation, and creation is what got us this far: to an age where many of your friends can be people you've never actually met, to a time where you can fall asleep in one country and wake up in another a few hours later, and to a world where each individual holds the power to craft something of profound significance that enriches the lives of themselves and countless others. To this tune, we are in a world, a world of *endless possibility*. ♪ ♫

"I see it, I see it, and now it's all within my reach... Endless possibility" – Sonic in Sonic Colors

Luckily enough, as the title of this book suggests: as you exist, and as you are human, you are built to create things. So, no matter if you feel you have indeed lost these adolescent senses, you won't have to dig too deep to find them again. All you really have to do to get them back is to start creating something, anything... which shouldn't be too hard because you know... *cough cough*... the title of this book... you were... *built to create*.

Rediscovering your long-lost creative senses is a matter of looking inside yourself. Looking inside to shine light on your genuine curiosities. Don't worry, we will discuss curiosity in plenty of depth in the pages to come.

What the heck does all of this mean? It's true that this book may feel abstract or far out at times. Well not even may: it will. And it will be until you experience the process of creation for yourself. It will be until you get lost in your own craft and curiosities because your own first-hand experience will be the best vessel to understand the words I've written here. Therefore, you will have to actually go and create things, not just read this book. If this book makes you create something, then I've done my job here well.

When someone is focused on creating something, they are in another part of reality; one where in the current moment, nothing else exists. The only thing that exists is the creation and the process of such. Anything outside of this is not just pushed to the side of the brain, but as far as the creator is concerned, for the time being, it doesn't even exist in their brain: almost like it's been temporarily erased. Creation briefly puts you off the map of reality to create new realities.

Of course, creation is not a mental disease. It won't hinder your memory, but there's not really a better way to describe the surreal feeling of focus while in a creative state. Consumption for most people is where their idle time lies and unfortunately, it's where most of their focus lies. This book aims to help weigh the scale towards creation, because yes: today most humans are overfed on consumption and *severely* lacking in creation nutrients.

Why do I want to tip the creation scales you might ask? Well, where we are today, it is only thanks to the people who chose to create even when they could have very well chosen not to.

If there is a key feature in a path toward fulfillment, it is not found in consumption, but in creation. We all create in different ways, we are all curious about different things, and we can all choose to create, even though we don't need to in order to survive. In the end, however, those who choose to create end up crafting the future in which we will soon live. Don't you want to be a part of that? Or at least *your own* future?

Throughout this book I will take you through examples of creators, how they benefited from using their natural gifts (that you have too) and how all of society has also benefited from their choices to create. Not every creator must change the world, but every creation does change someone's world [view].

My aim here is to convince you of course, that you will benefit from creating things and following your curiosities, whatever they may be. I will do my best to show you many pathways that others have taken so you can best create your own.

For the sake of things other than money, like the well-being of yourself and those around you, creation is a superpower that the world needs more people to utilize. I can't say that there is one moment my brain realized that this was a path forward for us humans, but I can tell you this: every day that you create something you will become a slightly better version of yourself and in the process increase the net consciousness of the earth beneath your feet. All of us humans have this choice, to create (or not to)

Creating stuff allows us as humans to:

- experiment with what we enjoy
- explore our curiosities and the world around us
- figure out what we enjoy most
- improve at what we enjoy
- share our findings, lessons and work with others
- find out what works
- find out what doesn't work

and complete all of the above with immense speed when compared to the speed it would take if we were just theorizing everything or stuck wondering "what if".

It's not hard to create things either, especially when you are following your genuine curiosities. You're probably already doing it in some sense and this book will help you find out what you need to stop doing and more importantly what you need to focus on in order to embrace the natural human abilities that you were built to use but sparingly do.

Before we dive any deeper into this book, I want to make it known that I am not trying to make you into anything that you are not. Rather I am simply expressing my own thoughts that hopefully trigger your brain into a state of thought too.

That is to say that I am only trying to get you to ask questions about yourself, to yourself. So you can see parts of yourself that you either haven't considered before, or have long forgotten.

If you feel that any part of my book does not ring true to you and your gut instincts: then it may be so that you are right, for I am just a human like you with many faults.

*You may also find out for yourself that you are wrong. Either way: wrong or right, it does not matter. What matters more is you allowing yourself to be a vessel for finding **your own** truth.*

*So, you may create great big things, you may create small things, you may create things that are not things at all, it does not matter. I only ask that you read this book acknowledging the notion that you have a choice: the choice to participate in the world, and the chance to add something uniquely **you** to it. This choice is simple: to create, or not to create.*

*Most of what you read will be my own experiences; almost all of it. Please note that **I don't have all of life figured out**. The two kinds of people who do are known as liars and fools. I do have a curious feeling inside of me that has guided me to write this book. And honestly, I think that's enough to warrant one, two or maybe even three people reading it. So if you're reading this, thank you. I only hope I can repay the favor by sparking some of your curiosity while reading the contents to come.*

Enough jibber jabber, let's get at 'er *(something my dad says from time to time).*

:)

If this book encourages you to create something, anything at all, feel free to share such creations with me and the world by tagging me on social media @jackfriks or use "#frikit". I would love to support you and your creations.

Or just DM me. Or email me jack@frikit.net

Feel free to share any of this book's contents or talk about it with other people. The ideas in this book are yours now too; I am passing them along for you and for others to enjoy their optimistic future and in order to create more cool sh*t. Thank you, my friend *one.*

You were built to create (cool sh*t)

"To create is to bring something into existence that wasn't there before." - Rick Rubin

Creation is an amazing thing. It's the reason you're able to read this book or any book. It's the reason you can type an angry comment on a Facebook video and it's the reason you can enjoy a week in the Caribbean ocean when it's the middle of winter and you live in the great white north of Canada.

Have no doubt about this: when I say **you** were built to create, I do really mean **you**. Not just your creative cousin that's super artsy, or your best friend that is always writing cool stories or doodling in their notebook. I mean **you** too. Whoever you are, whatever you may find interesting, there is inside of you the ability to create.

I also want to clear the air before we go any further... Creation is not a sacred action in comparison to other actions, it's just an action. One we as humans can choose to perform. Similar to how we can choose whether or not to get up out of bed and pee when our bladder is about to burst. You can choose whether or not to create, yes... **you**. Creation is just one of the many things humans are naturally built to do.

We are built to walk, fish are built to swim. Unlike fish though, humans have a real capacity for thinking, also known as *intellect*. Humans can use this brain power in many ways, but at the base of doing anything progressive, creation is needed. The term "creative thinking" is just that: creation in thinking. New pathways form in one's brain to solve new problems, to elevate one's experience, or to craft a new experience altogether.

Keep in mind that this book is not a prescription to tell you what you can or cannot create, or what you should and shouldn't create. This book's sole purpose is rather to showcase your own ability and let you figure out for yourself how you're best suited to use your natural creative abilities.

The main reason I'm telling you this now is due to the following examples I'm about to give. I will share with you people who have used their creative abilities to create great things; things that may even inspire you. One thing all of these people have in common is that they are all following what comes naturally and genuinely curious to them. Something I will talk about in later chapters of this book when helping you to get out of your own way. So you can follow a similar but completely unique route: your own route.

Every human on this earth, including you, can create awesome things and get lost in the process of a craft. By no means do you need to be a super influencer or online media personality to benefit from the joy that can be found in creating things. Now our first creator in question, you may know them well (you may not, that's fine too):

Example #1: **Your local school music teacher.**

Perhaps this is a bold claim to make, but I think it will hit more chords than it misses. Think about it for a second, before I tell you why your school music teacher holds any significance in their creations... The answer is that *they are playing their own tune,* and not only that: they are sharing what they know excitedly with others. For the most part, the people who end up being a school music teacher are those who feel it'. They're people who in some way or another find great depth in music. Whether it be playing it, sharing it, or creating it: they get lost in the process and in the creation of their current reality. In some way, all of music is a form of creation, but more on that later.

My partner's dream is to be a music teacher, quite funnily enough. Guess when and where I've witnessed her getting lost in creation or "in her craft"? When she is playing the piano or singing i.e. when she is creating musical sounds! There are many more day-to-day cases like this. At the same time, 99% of people are not devoting themselves to stopping the nasty consumptive habits that prevent them from experiencing these creative and fulfilling moments any more than a hybrid eclipse. And in my few years of earthly experience, I have yet to see such a rare eclipse come or go.

Example #2: **Nikola Tesla**

Born on July 10, 1856, Nikola Tesla may have had an easier time not being distracted when compared to today (the 21st -digital- century) but so did all of the other humans around him. Regardless, Nikola Tesla is a creator who followed what came curious to him and is the man responsible for many luxuries we take for granted today. Had Nikola Tesla and many of his fellow scientists not been such large proponents of creating things, well then... we would be some time behind in terms of the following:

Electricity in our homes, electric motors, radio and TV, lights that save energy, machines that take pictures inside our bodies, remote controls for devices, wireless communication (like cell phones), and ideas for charging things without cords. Yes, this example may be an oversimplification, but it is not unfactual either.

Example #3: **The community organizer**

This is someone who everyone will run across in their lifetime. This role is not for everyone, just as all other roles, but this role is certainly for someone. Someone passionate about bringing people together, identifying shared goals, and organizing events that foster a sense of belonging. The community organizer *creates* connections, fosters relationships, and uses her creative abilities to plan activities that promote more unity and any and all types of positive change. This can range from organizing neighborhood clean-up days to food drives, to festivals. Regardless, without a community organizer a lot of the events around you wouldn't have ever happened because they wouldn't have ever been created.

Example #4: **The do-it-yourself creator**

You likely have a hands-on friend, uncle, or aunt who thrives on DIY projects. They can turn a scrappy piece of wood into a polished piece of furniture, or transform a rather boring room into a cozy and inspiring space. Someone who would rather try and create with their own hands and fail than sit by the wayside of hiring someone else. This is someone who is constantly learning new skills and thrives in the environment of creating new visions for what is possible to craft with their own two hands... You certainly don't need to be this person to know they exist.

Example #5: **The pro chef, or even the home cook.**

Cooking is a craft, and in a craft, one can get lost. A cook is an experimenter first and foremost. Experiments are done by twisting an old recipe around, bringing in new flavors to an old dish, plating the food in a new spunky way and in the end: turning everyday meals into new experiences that can be shared (and devoured) by hungry family and friends. From the pro chef to the home cook, the person cooking foods and making a meal is a creator no matter the outcome. What may make someone a better chef or better at anything is simply taking up the chance to continue creating more things in a specific area.

Example #6: **The gardener, the plant mom and the plant dad**

Many people take up the hobby of gardening as they get older. I think a lot of this has to do with the fulfillment found in creating things, especially things that take as much effort as gardening does. People often keep track of the water they give their plants more than they do their dehydrated self. Someone who gardens may want their living space to look livelier, or their backyard to inspire them with their morning coffee. Nonetheless, the enjoyment of gardening still comes from the act of it; the act of creating something new out of what was once something else. In the 21st century, many older-aged humans are experiencing abundant retirement. As a result, in the absence of the daily fulfillment they once derived from their children or work, they now often turn to tenderly caring for the plants in their garden.

Example #7: **Loving families**

Families are not an easy thing to make, from the first baby to the last straw of dad's tolerance. The people who take the time to create loving families are not just creators I look up to on a deep level, but people I wish to embody as I grow older. As with many things which humans create, the big reward here is really the journey, not just the destination or end result. Even if at the time it feels less than fun, it's bittersweet to know you can nurture such a wonderful, irreplaceable thing: A loving family. This is something that requires attention, dedication, patience, and a whole lot of love. Some may call this a craft too, and I wouldn't be opposed to that stance. For certain, a parent and/or grandparent who has pushed love above all else is a highly esteemed creator in my eyes.

// I had many more examples here, but the truth is there are a near-infinite number of different ways people have discovered to use their creative abilities.

Enjoyment

Keep in mind here that the relevance to creation is not that we may find ourselves being paid to create what we enjoy most, but that we can enjoy what we create and the process of such regardless. In many cases there is an intense butterfly effect of added value to the world with each new creation, from the music teacher's love of music being passed on, to the love and empathy a gardener finds for others while tending to their plants. This goes to and from all the way to the invention of fluorescent lights. In each sense the world inherits the benefits of each creator's creations in all sorts of ways, even some that may not be known to us now.

Not all of us humans fall into living a life where we can wake up every day and dive into our most preferred craft, but we all have the ability to create in some form or another and do it in line with our curiosities. To forfeit this human gift is a sad thought, *don't you think?*

So with that being said, let us dive into the practicalities and methods that you can use to create your own path forward. As someone who does not want to leave your gifts of creation starved from the world, keep on reading.

two.

You + Creation

The world may not care what you do directly, or what you do/don't create, but there are a lot of people who stand to benefit a great deal from the formula that is: you *plus* creation.

"I'm an introvert by nature but man there are moments where I see someone put out their soul into the world and I love it, I absolutely love it, and I am here to urge that person to keep going, the world needs your creations, and if not the world, then I do. Go fuck some shit up." – Me, the author of this book you're reading now, taken from something I wrote, somewhere else.

Creation is not about convincing others but rather showing yourself the way forwards... for you. To express yourself *through creation* and *create cool (or hot) shit*. Not literally though. It's a figure of speech; there's no reason to alter the temperature of your excrement.

I know many of us have different creative genes, and even my own creations change from each hobby or craft. This is because being creative is natural for us humans. (there will be a whole chapter on this to follow). It is innate to us humans because whether you like it or not: *You were built to create.* To cook and create a meal, to connect and create friendship, to draw and create a self-expressed visual of our mind, to garden and create music, etc. etc. The list goes on, to near infinity.

I've written about creation a lot; the superpower of it (which you'll read soon too) and the point of why creation is so important in our mundane life. The life we live now where it's much easier to pick up your phone and scroll than it is to sit down and play the piano. The life we live now where we cannot simply go outside for a walk and let our brains wander in imagination. For many that would be too boring to endure. Reality shows us however that imagination is not boring at all, as it is really just a state of creation in its most pure sense of beginnings.

What is the goal of creating things?

As bland as it may appear, the goal of creation is simply the process itself. Therefore, the goal of creating is to *create*. I used to think the goal of creation was finding what makes you tick, or how you can express your internal being to the outside world. Part of that has some real truth, but in reality the journey is always more important than the destination. So yeah, the goal 'creation', like any infinite process, is to be in the process itself. Now... the benefits and reasons you may care about this goal? Those questions and answers are to follow.

Why should you care to create?

The reason, or reasons why you should care to create may be limited to your own world view. However right now I'll give you some things to ponder and perhaps you can come up with your own reason to give creation more of your attention.

First off: creating things helps you get a lot of the 'what if' thoughts out of your head. This is because creation pushes you to take action and action moves you quicker to where you want to go than the inaction often found in consumption. This action of doing things found more so in creation yields results because, as a wise man once said: *You can't make an omelet without breaking a few eggs* – and most people are afraid to break any eggs at all!

Creating things can also be similar to investing in a portfolio of stocks you see potential in but this portfolio is the portfolio of yourself. If you can see potential in yourself, then you can begin adding to your skills and experiences through the trials of creation and craft. An ultimate reason for caring to create may also be that you wish to bring something new to the world and the only way to do so is to *create* that something.

Finally, although this is not the end of the list on why you may care to create: You may want to create things just to be in the motion of an infinite game, one where the point of playing is to play. Similar to the journey being the point of travel, creating things is the point of creation and to be lost in this process is a wonderful thing – much more wonderful than to be lost scrolling through pictures of other people's food on the internet.

The evolution of things

In order to progress we must create stuff, and have failures. It is only when we fall short or fail in some way that we can continue to pursue our creations at a higher level with the lessons learned.

Applied to business this means that you may create a business and it may fail horribly, but the critical mistakes you make are kept with you on your next venture. Or perhaps a failed part of your business allows you to see the holes forming around you and in your business plan, then you can adjust accordingly. Regardless, you must create something to start with, i.e. a plan. Then from there: adapt and re*create*/re*craft* your plan after finding what does and doesn't work.

Apply this to life and you may realize the plans you create to reach your goals, or the things you produce don't always work the first time around. Being able to see the problem and then correcting the problem is the evolution of making progress in any area.

Apply this to technologies and you'll see how often iterations (or new "creations") are adapted: changes made -> problems found -> problems solved → changes made → and so on… Technology advances day in and day out. In this part of the world, creation and recreation happen faster than ever because it can be done through leveraged mediums like code and open-sourced developments where others share their failures or possible solutions.

The evolution of the things here in the 21st century is one where technology helps us leverage our creation abilities to new heights: heights that are only rising in stature. Now, back to our main questions…

When do you create stuff?

Many will ask the question in life "When do I do this clearly beneficial task that I don't feel like doing?" Waiting to feel ready is the bane of most of our existence, not limited to just creating things but in all of life's not so sexy tasks. Tough luck for us humans however because the unsexy tasks that we often avoid are also usually the most important tasks as they bring the bulk of results. So, pushing them aside is pushing aside any of your progress too.

It's easy to forgo these tasks with distractible tasks: scrolling on social media or doing busy work instead of using your mental cognition to get something worth its juices done. The action of creating things is not really an art form: it is simply you, sitting your ass down, (or getting your ass up) and just **doing the thing**. Creation will often require you put aside distractions to allow yourself to fall into the thing at your fingertips (the craft), and fully commit to it at that very moment. Yes, this is where the art form of your creations begins; only after you have first sat your ass where you must be in order to create what you want to see or be.

Creating things will not always be a hard task, but it probably is for you now. I suspect that for 9/10 people reading this, these ideas are moving against what is ingrained in our brains. Going against cheaply earned dopamine in the years of applications that have no end to their consumptive limits. Creating things is intuitive to humans, but our human brain also has its pitfalls and can easily fall prey to a lack of creation in our day to day lives.

If you were to abandon the death scroll or other non-creative distractions for some time you would likely find yourself bored a lot more. This gives you more time to think, and natural imagination will come about sooner rather than later to push you to create something. Your curiosities can't be bottled up forever; for most of us, they lay in wait, ready to be explored. All we need do is get rid of the noise taking us away from them, and there they lay. To close this question off: If you are going to ask when I think you should create, my answer is to create whenever you can... this becomes much more likely if you take away distractions that suppress your own genuine curiosities and intuition, even if it's just for a short period of time.

Two final questions you may have:

What do you create?... How do you create?

As per "What do you create?": It doesn't really matter. The universe isn't asking you to fit a mold or a job path; the universe doesn't care. Create what comes to you naturally. Create based on your genuine curiosity. This is at least how I would put the best way to find out for yourself what it is you should create. Be careful with this: I do not mean to follow what is always easy or what you feel like doing at all times, but rather to find what you're curious about and create things around that.

What would you actually be creating or doing if you didn't have mental hang ups on it being *hard* or worrying that it may leave a 'bad' perception of you to others when compared to societal norms. – Sidenote: the hard stuff is the best stuff. Your answer to the questions above are what you should probably create around. If you have no answers then you have more of your curiosity to explore, which is also an answer. You must create in your day to day life some *imagination*.

Now, *how do you create*? Well this is really up to you. There are an infinite number of ways in which you can create. I've mentioned quite a few leading up to this chapter; even creating memes is undoubtedly a form of creation. Heck, imitation is not only a form of flattery, but creation itself too. To create what those before you have already created holds no less significance in your natural craving to do something creative in nature.

There isn't a prescription for our creative genes because each of us are completely unique humans with different interests and views in the world, so the only real way to figure things out for you is to try. Not every seed you plant will bear fruit, nor should you expect all your creations to net you the same fruits. Take for instance the Pareto Principle.

The Pareto Principle

Also known as the 80/20 rule the Pareto Principle states that 20% of things one does are the vital few that brings 80% of the results.

Putting this into an example, let's say you have ten crayons, but you only use two crayons most of the time because those two are your favorite colors. Those two crayons are the 'vital few,' and the other eight crayons are the 'trivial many'.

You can now take it into account that a small part of what you do can have a big impact on the results. This way you can try to focus more on the vital few tasks that bring 80% of the results. It's as if you had to pick your two "most productive" crayons; *you know*—the ones that actually make up your finished work (the results).

Knowing the Pareto Principle helps you focus on the things that really matter. You can spend more time and effort on the 20% of activities that bring you the most enjoyable fruits (happiness, success, etc. – whatever results you're aiming for). This way, you can use your time more efficiently. In general, the Pareto Principle is like a helpful rule that reminds you to focus on the most important things and by doing that, you can make your life better and achieve more with less effort.

If you want to see this taking place in your life, then look back in hindsight at something you've spent a lot of time and effort on. You'll probably see that most of your results came from 20% of your efforts.

This also applies heavily to creations on the internet. Say you are a writer creating articles: the Pareto Principle can be applied in many ways. One way being that for every ten articles you write, on average two may end up gaining more substantial traction compared to the other eight that got little to none. Or another way to look at this is that 20% of the time you spend writing may actually make it to the final draft of your published work.

This principle isn't perfect, but it certainly helps to know of it in any case. Apply this rule as you will to what I've mentioned previously in this chapter; maybe the dots don't connect right now, but eventually, they just might.

*// Oh so encouraging, I know... don't worry, **you got this**. Example: wouldn't it be rather humorous if you created something that yielded you the 80% of results? :)*

Your final form*ula*

This chapter has been all about **you** + creation. "The formula we all need". The thing is here, and I want to make it very clear: **there is no perfect formula when it comes to creation** and there never will be a perfect way for someone to create that can be applied universally.

Rather the formula that I propose is one of getting into the journey: a formula for more fulfillment in your life and enrichment of those around you. You + creation = better life.

How do you get a grasp on the creation part of this formula? Well, that's up to you. Your options are only expanding by the day, so long as you give yourself some time away from constant consumption and take some of the ideas in this book to heart, you should fare quite well

two and one half.

Creation is in everything

This chapter is marked as "two and one half" and if you ask me why, I couldn't give you a logical reason: it just feels right to create it this way. Mostly, I think it's because the vibe I intended to put out in this chapter is different from some of what's to come. This chapter is my own personal brain dump from half a year before I started writing this book, and man, my past self has some important and useful things to say. I think you'll find it encouraging, so I'm putting it early in the book with the hope that you'll want to keep reading the following chapters..

To start it off, I'll provide you with a big F because yes, I give a lot of Fs (about you and other humans creating stuff).

For the longest time I've thought that most of society was doing things the wrong way, I never knew if it was me missing something or that perhaps someone was smarter than me. Until one day I woke up and realized that everyone around me is just human. A human created the internet. A human created the device I type this on and a human made the human who gave birth to me (who is also a human- *shocker*).

It only makes sense then, with logical deduction, that if one human can create something wonderful, something to be in awe of, another human is perfectly capable of doing the same.

I've been battling with an inner monologue of this idea for a while. What it boils down to is us, as humans, being built to create. We are built to create; you were built to create. This is what I've been chanting for some time now, after I came to the realization that it's what I've been doing all along. In my departure from the traditional path life laid out for me, to the one I am constantly in the process of creating, I've embraced this mantra.

Creation is not something I think most people understand either. It's in everything we do. I could list off any activity and tell you how it links back to creation in a multitude of ways but instead I'd rather focus on the meaning behind 'creating things' and how it benefits our lives in tremendous ways.

Creating things is not about making more money, achieving a higher level of social status and it's certainly not about your parents being less, *or more,* disappointed in you.

Creation surpasses all these hurdles and gets down to the core of the human soul. Creation means your brain is ceasing to think about all the bad, monomeric thoughts running rapidly in that thick skull of yours. Creation means new pathways are forming without thought. Creation means you're traversing your own unique pathway to whatever part of life you may be enduring right then and there, or here and now.

In creating things there are a few games people play. One game commonly played is zero-sum creation. People create something where they must make someone else lose so they can win. (1 [winner] - 1 [loser] = 0)

Zero-sum games are not much fun for all parties, nor are they enjoyable: they leave someone bitter as someone must end up a loser for there to be a winner. This creates a more spiteful world, and who wants that?

If you can, try to play games that are positive sum: [1 + 1 = 2] or [1 + 0 = 1]. Create things that help others without putting someone down, or create things that bring you joy without taking it from someone else. These are the most worthwhile creations and they aren't nearly as difficult to come by as you may think.

Of course there are exceptions to these ideals. In a competitive market, there will be… competition. That doesn't change the fact that you have a choice in many aspects of your life when you're creating something. You can take the route of addition, or subtraction. Choosing to add is more likely the better of the two paths, especially on a long enough time frame.

three.

A lesson from my grandpa on creation

In many parts of my life I've questioned if something is worth the effort it entails. Many times I've determined something is not worth the effort. For example: getting in a fuss about the car driving in front of me failing to signal and forcing me to press on my brakes. Getting angry in many such cases I've decided is just not worth the time, nor the effort.

On the other hand, there are what I would deem as 'serious matters'. The matters that involve doing something for the process itself. To put in effort to no tangible end or to try simply because one can. To create something, even though it would be much *much* easier not to.

Today I bring you a lesson on a matter which entails great effort, from my grandpa: rest his wonderful soul.

Passing along a message from 20 years ago.

Recently, I started reading a book that my grandpa wrote and privately published in 2003. In the first pages in my grandpa's book are his notes to thank people for helping him write it… in these notes were also a great lesson.

I always thought my grandpa to be a man who could play music, write music, and write words very well from the get go... but he mentioned in his book's first section that when it came to writing his book, he was not a good writer at all to begin with. He had to thank all the people who read through his 1500 page manuscript with a great many additions and deletions over the course of a few years.

A quote that comes to mind is this one from Seth Godin on writers block:

"Writer's block is really just fear of bad writing. If you're willing to do bad writing, then good writing will slip through — it can't be helped. When people say "I don't have any ideas," what they mean is they don't have any guaranteed-to-work ideas." — Seth Godin

My grandpa, without ever seeing this quote of course, understood that in order to write a good book he would need to write a lot of bad passages first. So he could filter out the good in 1500 total pages down to what turned out to be over 400 good pages of writing and story.

Even though he was quite far from good at first, even though he knew that the book wouldn't be able to reach millions of people in seconds like it could today with the internet, he wrote the book anyways... because somehow, or someway, he also understood what he stood to gain in the face of his own creation

The overarching lesson here is the idea that anything worthwhile or fulfilling is inherently hard. Another thing I realized reading the introduction of my grandpa's book is that he was very pro creation from what I could tell. His way of thinking, although I barely got to spend much time with him, was very similar to mine. And to what I can gather from my mom; we were both all for creating things, whatever they may be.

What is there to gain from creating?

Why would anyone do anything that required effort? Well, most likely because they felt they had something to gain, even if intangible.

The angry driver puts quite a lot of effort to show their anger on the road, honking their horn, pressing the gas, giving the driver that cut them off a thumbs down, or another finger. In this case: the angry driver is so angry that this relief is worth the effort of doing the aforementioned things.

When a husband creates breakfast for his beloved wife, this also requires quite a bit of effort... but what is there to gain? Well there may not be much directly for the husband but a smile from his wife. Perhaps the wife would express her appreciation, that fills the husband's heart: to be felt as useful, appreciated, valued. Therefore the husband will certainly put in the effort. Love goes much deeper and does more wonderful things than this, but that's a topic for another day.

The point I'm trying to make here is that when someone takes action and invests effort, there's almost always a benefit to be reaped—a benefit that wouldn't exist had they chosen not to act or exert any effort.

But... what is to gain from creation, if one is creating something just for the sake of itself? If someone is to play what may be deemed an "infinite game"? Well actually, believe it or not: there is a whole lot to be gained from the process itself, outside of any possible outcome that may result from such a process.

I'm sure you've felt it before, you were doing something that required considerable effort but it was enjoyable at that moment. Sure your brain was scrambling. Sure maybe you were even out of breath... but no matter: you didn't want to stop.

You're in a type of state that transcends worry about what comes next; you're not thinking of anything else but the task you're involved in.

This is a consistent state one finds themselves in when they are creating things– lost in the process– in an infinite game of sorts.

Creation fuels the soul through this high, but when times get tough there is another force at play. The matter pushing you towards longevity: fulfillment.

In the example of my grandpa writing his book, he wasn't a good writer to begin with, but he knew from his past creations that he was on to something worthwhile. He knew because he had experienced the feeling of creating something worthwhile before.

Creating music was hard, writing a book was hard, all of his creations required considerable effort, and he could have very well not created such things, but that is why he created such things. Because it is deeply fulfilling to create such things. And because they are his very own additions to the world.

What you have to gain from creating things in general is to experience yourself adding to the world, because no matter what: when you take the effort to go and create something, in those same moments you could have very well forfeited such efforts.

So thank you grandpa, for choosing to create a great deal of things: even when you very well could have chosen not to.

four.

Creativity over IQ

For most of my life I have been under the impression that someone with a higher IQ than me had a better chance to live a better life. I believed that they had by default a head start in which I couldn't make up for.

Recently as I'm writing this book, I came to the realization that the past version of me was terribly wrong. It turns out that IQ means very little when it comes to predicting the quality of someone's future life: fulfillment, success, wealth, etc.

As someone has since pointed out to me when it comes to one's future quality of life: "IQ scores are about as meaningful as those 'Which Harry Potter house are you?' quizzes." – I'm not sure I completely agree with this quote, but it holds a deep truth: the truth that we put much weight on things we never had any control over to begin with; as opposed to focusing on what we want to see more of.

The real indicator of someone's future "good life" is often seen through their level of creativity rather than their IQ score. Incredible news for the non geniuses reading this book, and even the geniuses: creativity can be improved upon and strengthened! Just like you can train your muscles to grow, you can do the same with your creativity. This means *we are in control of our own future more so than most of us think.* Especially if we were basing our future quality of existence on our lack of IQ points.

Some food for thought on this topic is the trials and tribulation of one of the "most intelligent" men on earth:

"Rick Rosner has taken more than 30 IQ tests, revealing his IQ is between 192 and 198, depending on how the tests define their scores. Before the allegedly second-smartest man in the world became a TV writer, he worked as a bouncer, stripper, and nude model. He famously sued the ABC network for a faulty question after losing Who Wants to Be a Millionaire? at the $16,000 level, but lost the case." - Reader's Digest

Yes, this may just be a single example, there are also many examples of high IQ individuals living a great life and seeing a large amount of "success". Heck I can't even tell you that Rick losing his case against ABC wasn't all a part of his master plan to deceive you and I from suspecting him of total world domination… but if you think about it for some time you'll likely come to the same conclusion as me: there is no single trait that will save us from all of our troubles. Not even a top 0.0000001% intellect. However, what can help push us to make forward progress is in just knowing that we do have some control in our own fate; that we can strengthen our odds over time, instead of throwing in the towel after taking an IQ test and scoring lower than 192 (Rick's level of intelligence).

Creativity is often found as a better indicator of future success over intellect because it shows that you can open your mind to unheard possibilities. Many highly intelligent people of the past often deemed modern medicine as witchery, but because one does not know what one does not know: the possibilities to be explored can only be explored by those looking for the alternate route. The highly intelligent human may pass up such possibilities frequently if they lack the creativity to imagine what has yet to be explored thoroughly.

Creativity itself is largely connected to the curious people of the world. To people who do not bother to seem smart, but would rather quench their thirst for knowledge with knowledge. Even if it makes them appear less smart, or even as a complete and utter fool. Growing up we have this curiosity baked into us. Everything is new and everything is a sight to be seen. We ask questions about everything without hesitation of trying to seem a certain way, the tiny humans of the world just want to know what they do not know! Oftentimes we lose this curiosity growing up, and with it: a lot of our creativity. This is to say that our fear of how we appear to others has overtaken our appetite for knowing, and with it learning new things that we have not yet explored.

The good news is that unlike our given IQ score, we can change our creative "score" dramatically to the upside. Sure you may be able to increase your IQ score a point or two every few years, but how much of a tangible result will come of such a thing? My guess is probably not much. When it comes to being more creative, and curious, the results you can expect to see as you increase these traits is of a dramatic magnitude higher.

I could tell you all the ways in which creativity brings you a better life, but the truth is there are not many ways in which it doesn't. Every area of your life is enhanced the more creative you are: from how you solve problems, to how you look at life. The more creative you are, the better your odds of making something good out of something well...not so good. The only way for you to confirm this though, is to give it a twirl, to see if increasing your creativity, or trying to, is beneficial to you. I could give you a 10 step plan to 'increase your creativity' but there are already enough of those out there. If you're curious about them, go seek them by all means. Today though, I'll only offer but a few sentences about "how to increase your creativity".

Here goes it...

If you want to increase your creativity it is simple really: You must explore your interests, which is really what you are curious about, and you must also ask questions that make you think. Questions that may often challenge general assumptions you have about the world. *At the end of the day: to be more creative is to develop a growing thirst for exploration and discovery.*

Also: Ask better questions!
""A problem well-stated is a problem half-solved" – Charles Kettering

How you may go about following what I've said above is completely up to you. I know my message here isn't all that actionable... If you want a step-by-step exercise for this: then be curious enough to ask: ask yourself, and ask the world.

Go explore or go discover the answer for yourself. To be honest, though I'm not sure there can ever be just one good answer, or one answer at all for these types of questions. "How do you be more creative?". Well, you just be as you are, without trying to seem to be anything else. - This is the real challenge, to not challenge so harshly who we already are.

This challenge is one we can still hope to tackle, unlike our given IQ. Which is why I have put creativity well above IQ, as creativity has not only far more potential to grow but by itself shows much more promise that one would explore what comes curious to them: and this to me is something I've found to be of great importance when it comes to leading a more fulfilling life.

// editing note: In 4 months, I wrote this 60,000-word book. Now that I'm editing it, I'm astonished to see that I (me) (myself) have written some of the words on this page. It's as if a better version of me takes over my consciousness when I write... My brain is rewired for a short amount of time. This is where I believe my creative genius comes to show itself, not that I myself am a genius by any means, but that from time to time as I put my head down and do the thing bits of a passing genius come by and let me borrow them for a brief moment. I think we all have some version of this inside of us and it's entirely independent of our IQ score.

five.

Craftsmanship

If you could name a type of person who can be looked up to by almost anyone, what type of person would come to mind?

For me, it's someone who gets lost in creating things, someone who can lose track of time working on their craft.

To me, it's the craftsman (or craftswoman). This is someone I can look up to always, for they have found something ~~they love~~ that fulfills them-so much that all else fades away in the background when they are involved with their craft.

In this short chapter, we're going to look even more into craftsmanship, **how you can find your craft**, and *why you just might want to* as well. This route of creation is *one of many*, and is by no means the only way to create something worthwhile.

Why your free time is not fulfilling

The noble pursuit of creating things may also be called "craftsmanship". From a woodworker to a writer on the internet, there is a deep sense of fulfillment to be had while one is focused on their own crafts.

This is because having a goal and having a depth of focus in one's life ultimately makes it a lot better, even more so than if a crafter (you) were to have ample free time: being involved in a craft would bring your life more happiness.

"Ironically, jobs are actually easier to enjoy than free time, because like flow activities they have built-in goals, feedback rules, and challenges, all of which encourage one to become involved in one's work, to concentrate and lose oneself in it. Free time, on the other hand, is unstructured, and requires much greater effort to be shaped into something that can be enjoyed." – Mihaly Csikszentmihalyi from his book "Flow"

Time spent on a craft or occupation is more easily enjoyable than free time because it is easier to find fulfillment in something with clear goals and feedback. This is why a lot of intensely spent free time consists of people playing games.

How do you find your craft?

If there was one absolute way to find your craft, I don't know of it. The truth is there are likely an infinite number of ways to discover your unique craft(s) by exploring what comes naturally curious to you.

On the other side of the same craftsmanship coin, you will also find that even the things you find more or less mundane can be turned into a craft as well: with you as the core craftsman.

So, you have two options or 'possible pathways'.

The first is the scenario in which you want to find what comes most curious to you. You search by trying new things and exploring what comes to your mind as interesting. Eventually, you end up crafting something through this avenue, and at some point, you get lost in the craft. For some this is writing, for others, this is smithing, for your grandma it may be crochet, you may find more than one craft too. The most fulfilling crafts are enduring journeys, where the joy comes from the act of crafting itself, as there's no definitive end for your mind to fixate on. There is just you, and then there is what you ought to do.

The second scenario is that you have something you do that you may not always enjoy, but you find it extremely fulfilling regardless. This is a more common pathway of the 21st century when there are much more dynamics to living a full life than just having food on the table or a roof over one's head. This scenario is found in more so "darkness". Darkness in the sense that it's not a go-lucky fun search party for one's passion or interests, but a revelation of fulfillment in one's occupation or paid craft, one that somehow for whatever reason reveals itself as a craft to get lost in over time, maybe even after years of being involved. Perhaps a craftsman spends their whole life in the process of crafting only to retire and realize where so much of their fulfillment came from.

This second scenario is much less "just do this" than the first, but the truth is if I can tell you exactly how to do something, then it's probably not worth your full attention. The idea here on finding your craft is that you don't need to find something that sets a fire in you 24/7 because no one has a fire in them 24/7. Some people have just **devoted** themselves to the craft regardless, because they know where it will lead their sense of fulfillment and actual fulfillment.

// Devotion is a very underused concept. Many people try to chase after motivation and discipline but they miss the mark. Something is always not perfectly right and they don't feel motivated enough on one day, and another day they aren't disciplined enough to do the thing they ought to do. Devotion is the counterbalance here, devotion ensures you are committed to something even when your willpower is empty and your motivation meter is at zero.

Why should you find your craft?

Hey! I'm asking you, why? Do you have any ideas?

Chances are your brain is stumped in some way when trying to answer this question. I know I'm the one who brought you here to tell you about the subject of craftsmanship, but I'd like to end this wall of text with something different.

You: answering your own internal dialogue. Most of us avoid the thoughts that scramble our brain all day long, distraction after distraction, but if you sit for five minutes and think about this one question, you may be surprised by your answers.

Aside from being more fulfilled, finding your craft can enable you to have a go at making your "life's work", something that you are constantly progressing at, or working on. Again, this is massive for our fulfillment in life, and fulfillment comes with a very large relative dose of general happiness... but you know what else you being involved in your craft brings? Crafts are lifelong games to be played and enjoyed. A life's work doesn't need to always be serious, it just needs to be for life; and you can have fun, for life.

It brings people from all over the planet together and sparks them to craft things too. Your crafts have a massive butterfly effect to change those around you and with the power of the internet, the entire global population. I know you've looked up to someone who spends endless hours on their craft before, and by looking up I don't mean just to the end result, but to the process behind the result especially.

You are a creator and a craftsman too, and if you're just realizing it now: then you better get on with it.

Additional clarification for this chapter which you may find useful:

"Some things are a job, others are a craft. The primary difference is not the task, but the enthusiasm and curiosity put into the task. The more engaged and interested you are, the more it becomes a craft." – James Clear

To find your craft: follow your genuine curiosity more often than not.

six.

Consumption decay

Creation over consumption is the basis of this chapter.

As with everything in moderation, consumption is not a totally negative thing. In the digital age however, consumption has an increasing cascading effect as technology progresses and oh boy, has it ever progressed.

The infinite creations of content that lay on the internet in the year 2023 are so overwhelming that it is hard to know not only where to start, but when and where to stop. Here then lies our modern problem: Once you dive in, it is hard to get out. Once you are stuck in this loop of cheap dopamine feedback you will also slowly be sucking away your creative abilities. Making consumption nowadays a double edged and crudely serrated sword.

The reasons for this aren't all known to me honestly, a lot of it is from experience. So here's what I can tell you about consumption, and its decaying effects on your creation abilities: The more times you choose to consume rather than to create, the less likely you are to create later down the line. In turn: you choose easy over worthwhile more times than not. You may often lose your way, and find that you don't really know what you want, a lot of which stems from spending so much time decaying your creative ability via consumption. Consumption in the 21st century is not only easy, but it numbs you from looking inwards, from being bored and sitting with your thoughts, and these moments of boredom; like when you're in the shower, are what spark your curiosity to shine through.

Before going any further I think this chapter would do more harm than good if I failed to mention that oftentimes we can find great value in consumption, it may even feed us in our creations to come. So what I'm letting on about is not that one should never consume, but rather that one should watch out for what they consume and how much they consume in contrast to how much they create. Relax sure, but don't forget about what you were built to do; to create.

Curiosity Consumption

When we are creating things it often comes from a place of curiosity, however curiosity often first strikes into us through the familiar process that is consumption. So, how can we utilize our curiosity when consuming and avoid the aforementioned consumption decay?

Well, there may not be a complete way around the effects cheap dopamine hits have on our will to create; however, there are a few things that may weigh the scales in favor of creation.

First, let me mention this again: consumption is not the devil vs. creation. It is actually a vital part of a never-ending recycling process. So I wouldn't say that we should all stop consuming completely; that would be like going back in time to stop your mom and dad from meeting, rendering the future absent of your very own existence, which would be a silly thing to do, just like it would be silly to never consume and only create things. The truth is, humans are also built to consume. The only problem here that I see is that the scales have tipped a bit too much towards consumption and left a rather large gap in our creation efforts.

To be curious is a wonderful thing. To follow curiosity to each of its ends makes up a large part, maybe even all, of the progressive change we have seen in humanity over millennia. In this regard one may find themselves consuming frequently and more often than they create to meet curiosity's ends. This to me is not the harm, the harm in consumption and the creative decay that ensues is from the mindless form of consumption. The form where one finds themselves scrolling endlessly with no aim but other than to feel good for a short moment through itty bitty, non lasting dopamine hits.

Delaying Decay

Decay comes consistently from a lack of moving forwards. The most common denominator in the twenty-first "digital" century of this is the endless scroll.

The easiest thing to do when you're bored or are presented with a hard task is to simply pick up your phone, or open a new tab on your computer and scroll. Or answer your texts, to do anything but endure struggle... This is where decay begins.

To consume as a delaying effect: is the decaying effect.

Just when you are about to create something new in your mind, just when you are about to make it up to the next step: you opt for consumption instead. You miss out on a lot of growth by opting for consumption. While trying to delay discomfort you've simultaneously enabled the decay of your creative energy.

And I'm sure you don't want to decay your creative energy, who would? So this is your reminder that you have a choice: to decay and delay, or to embrace the discomfort and be well on your way (to creating cool s**t).

An example from my experience

I have found more and more that people are endlessly scrolling on apps like TikTok. I have also found more and more that this is taking away from people participating in activities aligned with their genuine curiosities.

Sure, there is sometimes useful information or "life hacks" that pop up when one is scrolling on an endless scroll... but 99.9% of the time, people are opening the app to scroll because they cannot stand to be bored. They do not want to think, or even be the slightest bit uncomfortable with their present experience.

Take the shower for example, when you are washing your body and you are alone with your thoughts, this is the time you come up with those fascinating "shower thoughts". Some of them may be a little wild, or even outlandish, but they are the type of unique thoughts that come to you only when your mind is left to wonder. These are thoughts in line with your genuine curiosities. One could put these thoughts aside and never go any further with them, but what are these thoughts worth? Well, I'd argue they are worth a whole lot. Perhaps, to the many people addicted to TikTok, these thoughts are actually some of the most important thoughts they have throughout the day.

If we are constantly filling our downtime, or extra time with mindless consumption: how can we really expect to discover what it is we actually want from life, or how one may go about getting to where we want to go? The thirst for figuring out such problems isn't just suppressed by mindless consumption, it's completely blocked. The only time one may find time to think of such things might just be when they are in the shower. Your shower time is hardly enough time to sort through the 60,000 thoughts you have each day. Finally, as a shower thought: you don't need water dripping on your head to soak up the answers you already have inside of yourself.

How can we truly discern what we desire, how to attain it, or what makes us tick, if we persistently ignore everything that creates even a slight discomfort inside of us? How can we evade the life decay that is caused by this mindless consumption? Perhaps the only comforting resolution here is to embrace discomfort, a notion many numbed by TikTok are reluctant to submit themselves to.

I, prior in my life, experienced mind-numbing sessions of social media on a daily basis. Then I went on a trip to the Dominican Republic. On this vacation I tried going without mindless social media scrolling for the entire length (seven whole days). I deleted TikTok and similar apps: supplementing these things with reading on my down time or "bored time".

Oftentimes I would also just sit there and ask myself "What do I want out of life?", then let myself remain uncomfortable until I could answer the question with an actual, in-depth answer. During the first few days I had a constant urge to want to go on social media, but I read a book instead during these times, or I wrote notes about what was on my brain. Both ways I was forced to think, I was forced to proceed with intention, and most importantly: in both ways I was forced to sit in *temporary* discomfort.

Slowly throughout my vacation my craving for the dopamine hits that social media brought me faded. I started to realize more of what I wanted to work on, more of what I wanted to learn about and all together: I realized scrolling on social media wasn't pushing my life forward on any metric whatsoever other than having a shared chuckle with my partner from time to time.

The cost of mindlessly entering such apps is that we leave behind our genuine curiosities, we leave behind the good and worthwhile stuff that adds real fulfillment to our lives, like creating things, working on one's craft, or towards a worthwhile goal. We leave it all behind because it's uncomfortable to think about, and it's uncomfortable to think about because of how much more effort it takes than scrolling on TikTok while also bringing us much less pleasure at the time being. It can be quite boring at times to do the things you ought to be doing in order to lead a creative and full life. Not everything will be exciting.

After my vacation this habit of not using social media in my down time stuck for some time, overtime it's easy to let it back in: but now when I use social media it is done with intention (I still avoid short form videos like the plague).

I set timers and I set a goal for what I'm trying to move towards while on social media sites: I only browse text based sites like Twitter "X", or Reddit and for the most part: my intention on this is related to my creations of writing, so this solution may not be suited to you. What matters most here to avoid such a decay is not just about taking away your consumption addiction, but realizing how much more fulfilling it is to think through your thoughts. Go on a walk and just think from time to time. Forget the music, walk for 20 minutes and just sit with your own brain. A lot of your brain's biggest queries and overarching problems are solved by simply thinking to yourself *intentionally*, especially so on a walk outside. Making ourselves realize how it's really not all so bad to be a slight bit uncomfortable is an important step to curb the decay that is often onset but mindlessly consuming.

I'd like to add that one may still create great things and mindlessly consume from time to time, or maybe even regularly... However, the people who do create things, and make forward progress while also having a large consumption habit are the people who put creation first, as a priority. Note: priority, meaning that someone has sat with some discomfort and then decided on what matters most to them, what comes first in their day as something they need to use their time on.

For me this is writing: It is a priority for me to write for 1 hour each day. Sure I can go on twitter or reddit, but not until I have written for 1 hour at least. Even then I have things that are much higher of a priority than social media, so it ends up being me on a consumption mode for a very fractional portion of my day; less than 30 minutes usually.

// This ranges in seasons, sometimes it's an hour now, sometimes it's 15 minutes. The whole mindless consumption part is really the biggest battle. Building a discomfort/boredom "tolerance" helps a lot, and so does having built up a strong drive to get shit done, to be excitable so much so about the work you need to do you have no time to mindlessly consume.

The consumption decay I speak of here is not invisible to a lot of people in the situation of such decay... It's just a really tough thing to kick when it makes your brain feel so good at the time being, and with such little effort. Even when you are aware of the damage mindlessly consuming things can do, it's just so easy to keep going on the easy path. – small reminder and slight wakeup call: all the best, most worthwhile things in life... take considerable effort (and come with *temporary* discomfort).

I have no guaranteed techniques for you on avoiding this decay. What I can suggest above all else however is to follow what comes naturally curious to you. This is the best advice I have received and can only hope it helps someone else reading this too.

Finally, I'd like to mention that on many days I struggle with consumption of things that don't push me forward. I think most of the short form contents are brain rotting in all honesty: So, I've at least put those to the gutter where I have deemed they belong. Still though, the ease of watching Netflix with my partner, or adding another YouTube video to the queue remains. I still crave such eases in many parts of my day... The hallmark for when I cave however is based on one crucial factor: Have I gotten my critical tasks done for today? – Have I worked on creating something worthwhile? (to me). For me right now this means "Have I written in my book for 30 minutes to one 1 fully focused hour?". So yes, TikTok and other media platforms may be poisonous to your creative abilities, but what I've found makes up the bulk of forward momentum is just making sure you're getting the most important things done every single day. Going about determining those things may be increasingly easier if one is not constantly stimulated by the ease of instant pleasure and cheaply earned dopamine (TikTok, YouTube, Netflix, Facebook, Twitter (X), Instagram, Reddit, Etc., etc.).

Proceed with intention, proceed with curiosity, go create some cool shit, or work on some worthwhile shit.

six-point-five.

Focus on what you want

As a follow up to consumption decay and the idea of "put it away", "don't do this", "your brain is rotting" there is another line in which I'd like to toe with you...

Focusing on what you want to see more of rather than focusing on what you don't want more of. I first came across this idea in my early teens but forgot about it with haste. I stored it into the neverland of my brain. Since then however it has been resurfaced to me many times over by Visakan Veerasamy – *"Focus on what you want to see more of."* – this saying is plastered all about his writing and profiles on the internet, and oh boy am I ever glad it is. Let me tell you why.

Consumption is this nasty thing, it's taking away so much of your creative energy? right? This may be true, but what's the flipside? How do we take this negative "no no no, don't do that!" view and turn it into a "yes yes yes, do more of this!" approach?

We focus on what we want to see more of. (*duh you silly goose!*) [internal memo]

But how do you focus on what you want to see more of? Well the first part is taking note of what you like, what you enjoy, who you enjoy being around, who or what you get energy from, what you get excited about, what you are genuinely curious about. These things are where you could very likely divert your attention to instead of thinking things like "I need to stop scrolling man I'm such a bad person I need to stop this"

Instead you can take on the approach of "Oh man I really want to learn about this other thing, I should spend my time there instead" or "Oh man this book is so good I want to read more of it" or "Oh man I have extra time on my hands right now I should spend some time thinking to myself and sorting out my own thoughts!" ... You don't have to add "Oh man!" to every sudden spark like internal thought, it's just something I do (I have no idea why).

The point being that you can focus your attention on where you want to go, or where you want to be *without* focusing on what you need to stop doing so much. Instead you can begin focusing on living the parts of life you would be living as if you had already stopped doing the thing you wanted to stop doing. One last thing to mention is that it is probably more effective not to just realize what you want more of: but to visualize yourself already having what you want. This ends up helping you get to where you [want] to go by making you adjust your behavior and habits to where you need to be to get there. At least that's the idea of what – inhabiting your wants as if you already have them – is about.

This approach may work for you, it may not. I have no idea. There is no such thing as a one size fits all solution to these sorts of internal battles. That's why I'm offering two sides to the same coin here. Ambiguity in our own natures: that's something I want to see more of in the world myself. The acceptance that we may not all have the same answer as everyone else around us, yet our answer may still be equally correct.

This idea of 'focusing on what you want to see more of' transcends how we go about changing our habits. For me it has changed how I see the world, how I go about creating things, and so much more. I can only hope you will be as moved as I was in seeing the beauty of focusing on what you want to see more of. Perhaps I've done you a disservice by not being able to adequately explain how I see this concept in a positive light. Perhaps I should focus on what I can lead you towards rather than what I cannot explain with my own words just yet. Perhaps, *yes*, I ought to focus on what I want to see more of.

We all can create great things, but to focus on creating what we want to see more of is an even greater feat, and to me a worthwhile one at that.

// The above text may appear a little cheesy, if you think it's cheesy, then I implore you to laugh at me as opposed to feeling cringed out about it all. There is a lot more fun in laughter than there is in scrutiny. There is almost no joy to be had in a state of repulse.. So do not repulse, feel the joy! Laugh it up, and focus on what you want to see more of. Surely you don't want to see more disgust, right?

seven.

Explore your curiosity

The most successful people and the richest people in this world have one thing in common: They're all some of the most profound experts at exploring their curiosities. *Riches be damned:* the people who live the most full version of their lives are all explorers of curiosity in some way without a shadow of a doubt. No one gets anywhere without being curious really.

Elon Musk explores his curiosities profusely and unapologetically: creating some of the biggest companies in the world (and making some money along the way too). Jeff Bezos explored his genuine curiosity of selling books and expanded Amazon with his curiosities into an everything storefront. Steve Jobs had a genuine curiosity to make something great with the new age of personal computers and give it to the world. These examples may be widely known, but even at a smaller scale, almost anyone ever who has been a successor at living a good life got there from this same seed. **A seed of genuine curiosity**.

The local gardening business in your town likely started from one person's genuine curiosity as to how a flower blossoms... or from being curious about which conditions may be best suited for the growth of a wallflower. Taking this to the internet, the gardening blog with more than

100,000 readers a month started from this same seed... *not the flower seeds*, but a seed of genuine curiosity.

One day someone somewhere had a question, and they needed answers. No matter the question, they pursued the answers with depth. Why did they pursue answers with depth? Well: the answer is that they were *genuinely*, and <u>absolutely</u>, **curious!**

Your potential is hidden inside your genuine curiosities. Look around at the devices you have, the tools you use (digital and physical). All of them started with this very same seed. Matter of fact, everything worthwhile seems to grow from: planting this seed in good soil (diving into your curiosity) *plus* watering it well and often (making time to explore curiosities frequently). When you are curious about something you learn without being impatient, you learn simply to learn. To quench your curiosity is the goal. Therefore, the level in which you are curious about something usually determines how successful you may be doing said thing (there will be a whole chapter on this later on).

How to explore your genuine curiosities

In order to be your own success story you may want to understand what 'exploring your curiosities' actually means. And more importantly *how* you can actually explore them. The good news is that this process is built into us as humans, just as is our ability to create. We only need to push aside the things that are acting as a blockade to our true nature. Just for enough time to dive into what genuinely interests us, to explore the things that make our brains light up.

The 'bad' news? You'll have to stop scrolling on social media for a little bit. In general, you'll have to stop autopiloting to mindless tasks that give you a quick and easy hit of dopamine. I'm not saying you can never use social media again or that you can't eat chocolate bars anymore. What I'm saying is that in order for you to take part in exploring you must limit your distractions to be only ones worth your curiosities time. You have to avoid the autopilot to check your email every 5 minutes. You have to avoid the autopilot to open your phone and scroll when your brain feels the slightest sense of boredom or discomfort in the work you're doing.

On that note, think if you can relate to this: Picking up your phone to go check the weather and suddenly you're opening up Instagram and scrolling, even though you haven't even checked the weather yet!

This happens more often than any of us want to admit. I watched my friend do this right in front of me when we were trying to look something up on his phone, he opened up Instagram and lost track of reality before we could even find what we were looking for (we certainly didn't need Instagram to get our answers). All things like this where we autopilot to something so easy that makes our brain feel good in the very short term are blockages to our genuine curiosity. Yes, curiosity does well under serendipitous moments and can be developed from random interactions. But if we're being honest: there are a lot better ways to create serendipity in our lives than to scroll on social media. It's hard to grow in any real direction if the only direction you are going on a day to day basis can be dictated by the word "scrolling".

How do you explore your genuine curiosity? What's the answer?

Well, the answer looks a bit...
....

like ....

→ this.

It looks like the above because for a few seconds you were wondering what came next, exploring one line of text to the following line of text. Maybe that sounds a bit fluffy, but it's reality. / /*Reality can be quite fluffy*

When you take away the blockages to genuine curiosity and you're fully focused on something, you are in constant pursuit of finding what comes next. Suddenly an hour goes by, and someone calling your name in your own house can't seem to break your attention at all, not even an inch.

You explore your genuine curiosities by letting your curiosity live and taking away unnecessary distractions. Find books you want to read or topics you are interested in researching to help you get ideas. Act on those ideas in whatever means true to yourself and in totality you will be following your genuine curiosity.

You may also get ideas from your own existing scramble of thoughts constantly hovering back and forth in your mind, that works too. Get curious and *get* **going!**

Why you should explore your genuine curiosities

If you aren't yet convinced that paying more attention to things you are genuinely interested in is a productive or proactive undertaking... Then here are some more reasons.

Your curious benefit to society: Society is a perpetual machine that outputs all kinds of oddballs, weirdos, geniuses, and creators. All of the above may be even categorized as a single person's traits. Even if two people had these same traits, the same skills and hobbies even, none of us are a replacement for each other. We are all completely unique in our own ways. This is because, *and you may have guessed it already*, we all have our own genuine curiosities. Society benefits a lot more from people who lean into their genuine curiosities than people who don't. Simply because: people who aren't leaning into some form of curiosity are playing life on autopilot, doing menial tasks, or collecting up cheap dopamine more frequently than not.

People who explore that inner voice, or itch to go down a rabbit hole of interest: to try something and fail, to learn about why something works the way it does. These people conjure the stepping stones they can use to reach breakthroughs. These breakthroughs may only be internal, or they may leave a lasting impact on the external world around them (humanity). Either way society benefits from such people exploring. New things may not just be found when exploring but also further understood. In turn this expands the general human consciousness and enhances the earth beneath our feet.

Curiosity meets opportunity: I'll keep these next 2 reasons for why you should explore your curiosity short because you probably won't agree until you experience them yourself. These are from my personal experiences.

Opportunities are abundant when you're stirring the pot, when you're doing things in line with your curiosity and exploring that itch you have in your soul. These are the moments you create opportunities for things you can do, what you can learn, and where you can take yourself in life.

Throw a stick in the water and watch it ripple. Dive into your curiosities and watch the ripples of opportunity surround you. Doing things, especially things you are genuinely curious about, gives you a much bigger net to catch the so called "lucky" or "just by chance" opportunities with.

Curiosity as fuel for a better and more fulfilling life: Fueling a better life in my eyes means being able to remain true to yourself as often as possible. Not for pride not to feed your ego, but to remain fulfilled and satiated in a never-ending quest that is to explore what makes you curious.

Exploring your genuine curiosities won't solve all your life problems, but it is much more fulfilling and rewarding than it is to dive into your social media feed. A better life is crafted through iteration of what makes each unique individual tick and the best way to do this in my eyes is to follow one's sense of genuine curiosity.

Most humans have forgotten their curiosity behind in their day to day life, it often takes going to a whole new country to get it back. You can be curious regardless, through questioning what you usually don't question, or by exploring what you keep saying you will "get to another day". The choice is yours: If you shall unlock the potential that lies in your curiosities. No one else other than yourself can do anything for you here. Your curiosities are yours and yours alone. *Explore as you will, your time's a' ticking.*

eight.

Becoming a graceful idiot

A damned long time ago, it was a jester's role and life's purpose to make the king laugh. The jester, also known as the fool, is a master of finding the right thing to say at the 'wrong' or inappropriate time: to make people laugh. The jester slowly evolved from making the king laugh, to a role of reminding. Reminding the people around him that they are only human, life is all one big game, and it's normal to see many parts of life as idiotic.

The fool was a reminder of finitude. A reminder of how little it takes to turn one's natural state of living to a state of non-living. These ideas largely come from a famous philosopher Alan Watts.

Watts believed that the court jester's seemingly foolish antics often contained profound wisdom. By acting in unconventional ways, the fool could reveal the absurdity of current social conventions and seemingly bring out others' realization to a more flexible and human approach to life. Although many people thought the fool a fool, he was in reality far from being so.

How does this help you?

If you could be less worried of looking like an idiot or a fool: then you can spend a lot more time genuinely exploring the world and your curiosities. You can approach what you are interested in with a genuine spunk, as opposed to one in constant worry of "How will this make me look?".

None of us want to be an actual idiot or a fool. Sometimes this is just our temporary fate (which we can overcome). But most of the time we are more afraid of being seen as an idiot than we are of actually being one. It's an odd game we play with how we are perceived is often the opposite of our true nature.

You may miss something and have to ask a question. People may think of you an idiot for asking such a question, but a real idiotic move would be to carry on pretending like you know something you really don't. Like when we are in school and a teacher says some important information, we didn't quite understand it or hear it fully... the fool would carry on and hope for the best, that such information wouldn't be needed later. The non-fool would ask a question in the risk of looking like an idiot knowing this is the only path to not be ill informed.

This idea that we can look like an idiot to others while making an attempt of feeding ourselves knowledge, lessons, and information is what exploring your curiosities is all about. If you're afraid of people thinking you're an idiot more than you are afraid of actually being one, then you're fighting a losing battle. In being afraid of looking like an idiot you end up trying to traverse through your curiosity with chains shackled to each and every part of your body. These chains are made of the most strong material there is, no sword or axe can cut you free. It took me much longer than a few minutes to realize that there is only one way out of these chains: which is to use your key. Your key is your brain and *your brain* is well... yours. So, you are the only one who can set yourself free, free to explore your own unique curiosity.

Not being afraid of looking like an idiot, but fearing the deep void of actually being one, is a much better way to go about life. Perhaps you'll find your own finely tuned approach to being a graceful idiot (I'm still working on mine, *gracefully*), but more importantly than finding this tune is to recognize that you are far from an idiot in the scenarios people think you to be one. An approach of saving yourself (and allowing your curiosity to exist) is the direct consequence of stopping to try and save face from *appearing* like an idiot. You aren't actually an idiot just because people think you to be one.

Before we wrap this up, I want to present a curious question that's come to my mind as I've wrote this chapter:

Is 'not being afraid to look like an idiot' enough to be genuinely curious?

This question is ironic in the sense that you may find it idiotic itself. It's an odd question, I'll admit to that. But in trying to answer this question, it prompts another question: *What is really going on when someone is genuinely curious?*

// quick sidenote: I think the best use of questions may often just be to prompt for more questions, so not every question has an answer, but at the very least: every question has some sort of path to be followed.

What's going on, when someone is genuinely curious, is much like what happens when your stomach rumbles to signal it's time to eat *"I'm hungry! Put some food in your mouth and don't stop until we're properly satiated!"* your stomach says. Curiosity works like this too. You are existing in the world and your brain is paying attention to certain aspects around you, it wanders into different thoughts and oftentimes you see something and your brain says *"Hey! I want more of that, we need to know more about that! Go inquire!"* – this is your genuine curiosity. There may be a number of reasons why you're curious about something in particular, but the brain's thirst: *to know more,* is there regardless, and if you're too worried about looking a fool, or saving face, then you will starve this part of yourself. A part of life that makes life oh so wonderful. The part that lets you create things in the world.

As you may imagine yourself trying to move forwards, I'll leave you with these two prompts:

Would you be more concerned with trying to avoid looking like a fool, or would you risk your appearance in order to inhabit the traits of the person you were attempting to only appear like?

"If a fool persists in his folly, he can become wise"

nine.

Just get started

// Recently I've been thinking a lot about what makes doing hard things so hard, & I've come to the conclusion that it's because the barrier to entry "Just getting started" seems so insurmountable.

In realizing this I've also realized some ways to pass this barrier, I've written some of that here in the hopes it may help someone else.

"The best time to plant a tree was 20 years ago. The second best time is now." - Chinese Proverb

Just getting started is the hardest part of doing hard things, so if we can find a way to just get started, then we can find the pathway to doing hard things.

This is odd... because in reality: it takes no more effort to keep going than it does to just get started.

In life, hard things are inevitable. For each of us, what constitutes as a "hard thing" may be very different. For some of us it's getting out of bed, for others it's walking up to a stranger and starting a conversation, for you maybe it's that you just can't start that project you've been meaning to for weeks now.

Luckily for us, I don't think life is really about being a master at doing hard things, rather it's more about being a master at: *just getting started.*

Getting past the massive amount of resistance that stands between you and the thing you ought to be doing. This is what life is about mastering, which turns out to be you giving it a go for just a mere minute. I'll discuss in a minute the value of doing hard things, even when they don't yield tangible results. First though I want to further discuss the possibilities behind getting started, how one may go about doing so for specific tasks, what you stand to gain from just getting started, and why getting started is the hardest part of doing anything even though it requires no more effort to continue than it does to just to start. Note: If we can understand how something works and why it is this way then we will be much more likely to overcome any obstacles it lays in our path: i.e. Getting started on our "hard things".

How to "just get started"

As I mentioned above: getting started is the hardest part of doing the hard things in your life. How one may go about tackling this task of getting started can differ from person to person or thing to thing... With that being said, I'd like to offer some practical examples for getting started on a few hard things, most of which contain telling oneself *a little lie*.

For example, let's say you are having trouble tackling a project that you've been wanting to do for some time now but you can't seem to pick it back up. You know it will take considerable effort or discomfort to get your brain back on the right track, the track that the project needs you to be on. In your head this is a monumental blockade just to start. If you had less of a brain perhaps it would be easier, but you have your brain in its entirety for better or worse, so we need to trick it. Instead of thinking about how daunting this task is, tell yourself you are just going to revise what your project's goal is, or something miniscule in relation to *kinda* working on the project without fully telling yourself you're going to work on it. A little white lie perhaps, because in reality you usually end up just getting started and now you can just keep going because you've come to realize the effort to keep going is not any higher than the effort you've already expended.

This doesn't always work, but it works a lot of the time. Even someone who knows that it takes no more effort to start than it does to keep going will fight this same battle consistently. Whatever your task, do the bare minimum of the hard and see where that takes you. If you need to tell yourself small white lies about what you are about to do to make it easier for you to just get started, then do so.

Why is it important to get started?

Although it may be obvious as to why it is important to "just get started", seemingly most of us don't take it seriously to do so. Honestly I'm not entirely sure why this is, maybe it's because of the news, or social media, or too much processed foods. Nonetheless I suspect the reason why people don't take getting started seriously is not because they are oblivious to its importance. Rather it's because they would rather be subject to stay exactly where they are than experience any "unnecessary" discomfort.

A common question people ask the people who drink coffee black or without sweetener: "Why do you like to drink something that tastes so bad?" The answer, at least for me, is because: if you start your day off with something that's bad, or makes you a little bit "uncomfortable" then your day can only get better from there. Better in the sense that the hard things to come will be easier now because of that cup of bitter swamp water you just drank. This is also known as "eating the frog".

But why is it important to get started? Why should you take your first lick of that frog leg, or drink that first sip of bitter swamp water? Well, because, as you already know, getting started is the hardest thing for our brain to overcome. So if one can *just get started*, then there's no telling where they will find themselves next (usually in a much more favorable place). It is critical for anyone looking to create something great or really anything at all that they just get started, and the sooner the better.

Why is getting started the hardest part?

Our brains like to make things seem harder than they are. This may not be true for all hard things, but for most modern dilemmas like "I can't get out of bed", or "I can't get in the habit of going to the gym" this applies well. Even for harder things that are **really hard** our brain will build up so much pressure that it seems impossible to just get started. You've been thinking about the pain of getting started all day long, of doing the whole task, rather than just taking the first step. This is why getting started is so hard: because most of the time our focus is not just on getting started, it's on step one, two, three and all the way to step fifty-four before we've even gotten out of bed we are worrying about the effort it's going to take to make dinner later. No wonder just getting started is so hard, we naturally are not taking it one step at a time, and as a result we are overwhelmed with all the frogs we are going to need to swallow throughout the day ahead.

This way of thinking gets us paralyzed in thought. To attempt to reverse this: read again what I've written above. Or if you can reverse engineer a way to trick your brain into only focusing on the first step (just getting started), then continue with that.

At the end of the day, all you need to really worry about is just getting started. Even then though, you need not worry too much, because once you are started you will find it easy to keep going. The playbook? One step at a time + Just keep swimming.

ten.

Creation is innate

"Every act of perception, is to some degree an act of creation, and every act of memory is to some degree an act of imagination." — Oliver Sacks

Creation is not only what humans are built for, but it has become inevitable that any human existing on earth will fall into creating things. This is because: creation is innate to us just as much as it is for us to learn how to walk. It is a part of everyday life, and even without intention, any human who breathes will find themselves creating things.

To *just create things* has been a long part of humanity's uprising, whether we know it or not: all of our achieved progress to make a better path forward has come through the hands and minds of human creation. Exploring ideas, testing theories, finding ourselves, getting lost in a task, or just trying to come up with a better solution to our own problems... all of these different ways to create things have gotten us here, to where we are today. I know this may sound cheesy to you or it may sound like I think that someone who creates things will find all of life's answers. It is not this way, for I know that no one will ever find or have *all* the answers, matter of fact, that's one of the very few things I know well.

There's this bell curve about life that one thinks we ought to do anything but "just create stuff". To think we must do all of these top one-thousand life hacks to live a full life, and we mustn't do certain things, taking a warm shower, instead of a cold one; for example, or we are doomed for all of eternity.

This is the absurdity that walks around contradicting itself day after day, that life must be complex, that we must adhere to all of the oncoming tips and tricks thrown our way. The truth is: the best advice, the best things in life are simple. So simple they are often found as boring, because: they are! But boring is a surface level quality to getting started. When it comes to implementation of boring things: we will often see that the side effects are far from boring, they are *exceptionally* enjoyable.

Creating things every day for example may seem boring, or like it requires a lot of effort. Me telling you to "create things" as a way to enjoy your life more may seem kinda boring… but what's to come of it is far from boring. The same goes for eating clean: the best advice to be healthier is to cut out processed foods, eat lean meats and avoid added sugars: this is simple advice, and it's also quite *boring*. No one is going to guarantee any part will be easy or fun, but what can be assured is how much better you'll feel afterwards. How much clearer your brain will be. How much less tired or groggy you will feel throughout the day, and how much clearer you are able to think. All from following some simple and boring advice on eating clean. I'm not suggesting you have to follow a super boring and super strict diet to make the most of life, not that it would hurt… I'm only making an attempt at showing you that the boring advice is also oftentimes, incredibly effective.

Sure you could hunt for the next lifehack on how to feel energized all day long. Ironically though, the results you find will just come back as scraps of the original "boring" advice. "Eat these 10 superfoods to become superman." =

Eat less junk and supplement snacks for fruits and veggies: *Boringggg*, but *effective*.

To just create stuff as it comes innate to you, and not think much of it. I believe this would be a great deal more impactful than to lead a life of constant intentional consumerism. Some may call this a boring life, others may call this a life of extravagance.

The simple things in life are not any less important than the complex, it's likely the simple things are even more important, most of the time. So if you're looking for the next life hack that will change your life: try something simple... try creating something; it comes to you naturally anyhow.

Coming back to the quote at the start of this chapter: "Every act of perception is to some degree an act of creation" - so it shouldn't be too hard to create something new today, right? A new way of looking at things perhaps. A new way of looking where you are and where you want to go: you can create that.

eleven.

Being a purple cow

"Be the purple cow in a sea of brown cows" — Seth Godin

// This chapter was for those concerned with striving for excellence, or to be exceptional in one area. If you aren't into that, then feel free to skip reading this chapter.

// editing edit: I decided to skip this chapter for you by removing it from the book. It was about 1800 words too long. See the below ending conclusion:

Some things you may be better off keeping as just a hobby or a side project. There's this weird place when you find a hobby you really enjoy (even if you're bad) versus trying to make it into something that yields you money or status: oftentimes it spoils the good milk in a way you can't get back from. To do things for the sake of themselves is a large component for enjoying creation and other meaningful tasks.

twelve.

Creation as a superpower

This short chapter is something I wrote a long time ago, well before I knew that I would be writing a book titled as this one is. Nonetheless, I think it's great (slight bias).

How is creating a superpower? What makes what I can create different from what someone else can create? If we can all create then is creating things a saturated thing to do?

Trying to answer these questions yourself allows you to see things in your own view before I tell you mine. Asking then answering questions using your own thinking is a large part of the creation process too; for expressing what you have to offer the world.

The first part of what makes creating a superpower is the process of creation over consumption. Consuming things is fine, but when you don't exert your ideas, your "what ifs" or even your urge to put a funny mustache filter on your dog, your brain becomes quickly overloaded to the point where you go on a sort of autopilot

Creating things allows you to break out of autopilot, and test for yourself not only what you enjoy, but how you enjoy things. Imagine if everyone created even 1/4th of what they consumed, the world would have tenfold or maybe even 100 times more data and knowledge collectively of human experience and progression than it does now.

Much of the reason people don't share their creations or go as far as to destroy their own work, is that we are so worried about other people's thoughts that we cannot express our own.

I'm not saying creating stuff is a miracle drug that will fix all your life problems, but I am saying that you will be better off creating more things in your life. Getting out of autopilot, learning more, documenting more, and sharing more in life than you would be scrolling on TikTok every morning. Rather: write in your journal, write a blog, make funny memes, take a picture of the sunset, send it to your family... There are many parts of your life that if you were focused on creating more and consuming less would be enhanced, maybe even all parts in a butterfly effect sort of way.

thirteen.

Creation vs progress

The topic of this chapter to me seems very niche, almost like I've never heard someone speak on it before. Nonetheless, I hope by putting my thoughts here some more people will discuss it: so here I am on a breezy Friday morning, creating this book and this chapter in it, ironically enough: with progress in mind.

I have on many occasions mentioned how *creation* is the reason humanity is where it is today: electricity, modern medicine, your existence, and the list goes on. With that in mind, you may be thinking that I am all about progress when it comes to creating things. But that would be wrong. In fact, a lot of creation I would argue should not pay mind to progress but should be enjoyed for itself. No matter if tangible results come or not.

Creation itself naturally brings enormous progress to human evolution, but some things creation also brings to the human experience are things like fulfillment, enjoyment, pleasure, carefree *fun* (entertainment for your soul), exploration of curiosity, a sense of self, connection, self-expression, and finally, creation is the best exercise for strong mental cognition (Creativity over IQ).

I'll dive more into progress in this chapter too, but first: who would be the people benefiting from creation without progress? Or how can you?

The answers to both of those questions lie in examples from the everyday of life. You may not know *how* you will use creation with an absence of progress, yet. But you're likely to figure it out soon enough.

First, let's think back to an example of a creator: your local school music teacher. Here we have someone who is sharing their deepest creations with a bunch of kids. These kids may not be all that into it, at least not as much as the teacher is. Some of the kids though are deeply enjoying themselves in the music. They may not be taking it super seriously or planning to play professionally, but they're creating music and simply *enjoying themselves*. This is creation without progress. The first example I'm giving is about more adolescent humans because this is where creation without progress is most common; or at least without progress in mind; It may be a parent's objective to make a child make progress over creation.

Now, outside of adolescence: I would implore anyone to take up a hoppy without progress top of mind. It's a wonderful thing to just do something you find fun, without progress in mind. To be professional in one area and a goof in another. Not worrying about progress is a great thing because it gets the human out of the way of their own treachery. It gets them out of their own way of always having to be proactive about going somewhere or getting better. Perhaps we can be better by being able to enjoy something for itself, what do you think?

Another example of someone enjoying creation without progress is in the creation of new adventures... Many people take up the arduous hobby of hiking. They map out an adventure, create a plan, and get on with moving their legs. Most hikes are long, tiresome, and get you to somewhere you didn't really need to go (little *progress* is being made). Despite these things there are millions of people who absolutely love to hike, walk in nature, and traverse steep inclines for the sake of themselves. Most people hiking also aren't training for a marathon or trying to increase their times on how fast they can run a mile. These people are creating adventures without progress in mind, they are taking part in a task where doing the task itself is reward enough. Perhaps it's not even a reward at all, but progress could be nowhere in sight and the human-turned-self-acclaimed-hiker still hikes.

This phenomenon of doing hard things for the sake of themselves isn't the only way people outside of adolescence enjoy creation-related events without progress either, far from it. The list could go on another mile, *or ten..* Or to the moon and back (not that I'm keeping count).

Take for example your grandma (or someone you know) who has taken up the practice of something like crochet. To crochet means to hook, and that's really it. A repetitive progress of creation that someone can get absolutely lost in making things: their own patterns, new patterns, old ones. This task is certainly one for the soul. The making of textiles using soft materials, to some boring, and to others impossible to put down.

You may be curious as to how someone can do something you find so boring for so darn long. This one crochet beginner I ran across on the world wide web mentioned they had fallen obsessed with crochet, they couldn't stop thinking about it, for 12 hours a day or more, they couldn't stop. To me it's the person who gets a high of something deeper (or less shallow) than the everyday buzz, they get a hit of something that they can get lost in, and in doing so are enthralled with themselves and the task at hand. For some people this creation-based activity that lets you express and find yourself is crochet, for others it's piano, or maybe it's writing fictional stories, maybe it's a mix of a few different things, who knows!

There's really only one way to find out, and it's not by scrolling on social media, that's for certain. One must explore their own creation abilities by some means. I believe curiosity is your best friend on this front.

Whether we know it or not, we live surrounded by many cases of people creating things, and creating them without progress in mind. To this tune these creators also reap a grand benefit, the benefit of escaping the constant buzz of the world and finding themselves.... where they had not yet had the chance to look.

Creation without progress brings humans all over the globe many benefits. For the kid playing music and having a blast in school: they are expressing themselves, enjoying themselves, finding themselves, and connecting with others through their own unique tune. – this seems much more "progressive" to me than scrolling on social media ever could, and it seems that way I think, because: it is!

The hiker benefits from creation without progress through sheer enjoyment of the activity (arduous as it is to hike), forming a connection with fellow humans; who are also in deep agony from that mountain they just climbed, and who couldn't ask for a better sense of self than the sense found when one is walking outside. On top of these benefits, there are many others that each individual hiker may experience. Some may not be notable or tangible to those around them, to the creator of their adventure however, the benefits are greatly felt, even if only in spirit.

Harnessing progress in our creations

Progress is by no means an evil thing. Now that I've told you how you can create things with progress out of mind (and reap the benefits) I want to discuss how you create with progress in mind (and reap some more benefits).

To use progress as a driver in your creations rather than a hindrance you will first need to understand how progress not only works, but also how it's made, and how it will feel in the reality of creating great things.

How progress is made

Progress is made by putting in consistent and persistent effort.

In this way, progress is made more frequently by someone who puts aside some sliver of time every day than the person who puts aside a few hours every few weeks. This is because daily effort compounds into progress much more efficiently than scattered effort.

Consistency is the most efficient way to make progress for two main reasons:

First, consistency makes sure you show up and put in the work. Without *doing the thing,* how will you ever progress?

Secondly, consistency keeps any problems that arise and stores them in your subconscious thoughts. When you do something everyday it ends up being not only in your active thoughts but in your thoughts while you sleep or when you aren't consciously thinking. The 60,000 thoughts you have each day without thinking too hard suddenly work to solve your problems and answer your questions as you go. Turns out: this is a wonderful way to make progress more efficiently.

Consistency is by and large: the laying of rails for your default train of desired progress.

Note that *focused effort + consistency* are the largest part of sustained progress, not necessarily how much time you spend doing something: but rather the level of consistent **focused** effort you put in.

How progress feels

Progress feels like struggle: this is a good thing. Struggle is a sign of progress.

The "hard" part of making progress largely comes from not being able to see progress as it happens. Progress does not show itself in many ways until you get over what feels like a lack of progress.

Many times I have become sad, or demotivated that I "just can't get better" at something, something is blocking me from leveling up. This frustration however is almost always the feeling we have right before we make a wave of progress.

What I've learned to be quite true is simple:
struggle = growth, and growth = progress.

A lot of progress feels like crap, but once you flip the switch of knowing what struggle really is, you see it as progress. It suddenly feels a lot better to struggle when you know what is really going on: you're growing where you want to go.

Creation based progress

Now, relating this to creation is a weird pickle. On one hand I'm prompted to reiterate that the benefits of creating things is largely about being in the process itself, but I also cannot deny that many creations have been iterated on with painstaking time and effort, which was probably not so fun to endure.

Progress is not always needed as I've mentioned before, but progress does push for greatness in creation. So if you're looking to create something great, then progress is your best friend. If you're looking to create something that brings joy to yourself and possibly others around you: then progress is hit or miss. Sometimes it may be useful, maybe you want to make progress for whatever reason, other times it's a hindrance that can stop you from doing the things you ought to be doing. Progress can demotivate you from creating the things you enjoy creating for their own sake. So take note now that you don't always need to take note of progress. You'll figure this out as you create more things, I have little doubt.

fourteen.

You have enough time.

"The myth is that there isn't enough time. There is plenty of time. There isn't enough focus with the time you have. You win by directing your attention toward better things." – James Clear

Today (Year 2023) time is plentiful, and it will only become more plentiful as robots take over our mundane works of life (like driving). But what is more scarce, and more important than having time? *Having **focus***.

Truthfully we don't really need more time to spend. We have plenty of it already. What we need more of is focus, to make our plentiful time count, and to make it mean something. This chapter is a brain dump on how I've learned to focus more on what matters and how it's changed my life [for the better]. // Doing the work, and focusing allows you to get things done much more efficiently, but this is a muscle that must be trained and kept in good health. It is easy to let your focus slip, so it's important to find what works and keep doing that.

In the 21st century focus is becoming exceedingly rare. Even if one had all the time in the world, if they don't focus on what matters most to them, time may not feel very well spent, not at all. I've come to this realization lately, and been attempting to adopt it daily.

Here's what's worked best for me (and may work for you): First in order to gain focus you will need to put the distractions away. This was nearly impossible for me at first and I'm still no angel, but the biggest step in saying no to scrolling on social media was having a strong reason *not* to be on social media. I did this by defining what I really wanted from life in all areas "What do I actually want out of life?" - Is now a question I ponder frequently.

You may find at first... it's a tough question.. It may drive your brain mad. Answer it anyways. Sit with the uncomfy. I answered this question in terms of where I want to be 1 year from now, setting goals for my business, health, relationships, and mind. Then I broke all of my goals down into tasks and highlighted all the things I could be doing on a daily basis to push me closer to each goal.

As it turns out there is **a lot** I have to get done. At first I thought "I have no time to waste!" but... after a week of trying to act each day and scraping by, I realized it wasn't a time problem, it's a focus problem!

Now having clearly defined tasks I can focus on what matters much easier. After you have clearly defined what you want, it's a lot harder to direct your focus to mindless scrolling or other because most of your focus will lay on where you're aiming to go. Still though, there will be a monkey up in your head telling you to "just check social media, really quickly". For the record: this monkey's noise takes a long time of redirected focus to be turned down.

This is inevitable, and I still have such a monkey in my head, so I needed another technique to be laser-focused at times in the day where I then can maximize my time to progress on goals.

What worked for me

I found a strategy called deep work in a book I was reading called - "Deep work".

I started to try some of these deep work sessions. First I did 25 minutes of concentration on **one** task at a time. My main focus was writing. The first 5 minutes were a little difficult, but after 10-15 minutes something weird happened. I became lost in my writing. I entered the zone. I was absolutely focused on the task at hand and time was lost in the milky way to me for those brief but highly productive 25 minutes.

Now maybe this is a small exaggeration, it's not always like this. But the only time I've felt this is when I'm dialed in; when I'm truly focused, when I have no distractions. When I set an intention and I do the thing, or get to work.

Pairing deep work with strong goals for your future has been amazing for me. I've found that I do have enough time, I just lack a lot of focus. There have been so many times I can recall not focusing on what matters and using 3-4 hours of my day unfocused. If I'm focused I don't need nearly as much time at all.

The gist of this chapter:

- You have enough time
- You don't have enough focus
- Figure out what you want to focus on
- Focus more on that.

Become a master of time --> remember that your time is still finite, *you're not immortal* <-- **focus up**.

fifteen.

The real creators (you)

A lot of the world in the twenty-first century has been focused on creating, just as the world in our many centuries before. However, In this current point of the twenty-first century; the one that I write this message in (2023), the term "creator" means something different.

To be a creator has turned into a trendy label. It's turned to mean: someone with influence over others, or someone who has leverage on the interwebs. Sure, someone who writes, speaks, makes videos and has a general presence on the internet can be deemed a creator... but to limit the term "creator" to this group of internet people is a malpractice of the word in all of its truths (in my less-than-humble opinion). To have influence is not a bad thing, but to think that you cannot be deemed a creator without it is a load of rubbish. So right *now*, I want to double check you know what makes **you** a creator just as much as any other human on planet earth (the floating rock we currently, exclusively, inhabit).

Your natural ability

You were born with the ability to create things. It's just the truth of our mundane matters. The matters in which we seemed to have pushed to the backburner. All of my life I have somehow known this in my head, and I think you know it too: we just fail to follow through with doing things we don't yet know how to do (because we never try).

Our natural abilities of creation go far past just being able to phone a friend, cook a meal, or plant and harvest some veggies... your creation abilities know little boundaries. You, yes: **YOU** have the natural ability to create new things, things that weren't here nor there before, what more could you ask for?

// Whatever more you could ask for, I'm sure you can cultivate it's essence in one way or another: so long as it's not asking to change the past

So yes: you are a creator, even if you don't have thousands of fans or followers: The absolute truth is that you are a creator by the nature of your very existence. Your unique existence is by itself something new in the world. This is a short blurb of text that you've probably heard before, but I think reminders are oftentimes more important than more new information or platitudes. Go create my friend.

sixteen.

The usefulness of chance

How I think the world operates, or at least: how one may encounter progress in the world, is kind of like this:

You *by chance* find something you're interested in; something you're curious about. *By chance* you end up spending a lot of time on it: learning, thinking, doing. Then by another *chance* you decide to devote yourself to it.

It's all really a rather large chance that anything is the way it is. By chance you've made it to where you are today, reading this now. Who knows what's to come of each and every big loss or win. Maybe each chance leads to nowhere, maybe it leads somewhere: it's really hard to be certain of any chance going any specific direction: but this can be a good thing...

At the end of the day, everything is a causation of some degree of *chance*. Let's talk about it!

How is chance useful?

If you think of chance as an *opportunity*, then you think of it as: who knows where my next "*by chance*" moment is coming from, where it may take me, and at any time in any day your entire life could change tracks. Leaving things to chance is not always about letting go of control, but more so it's about seeing where things naturally fall. Because maybe the way you wanted them to fall wasn't favorable to you after all.

Similar ideals of chance, the story of [The Chinese farmer](#):

The Chinese Farmer Story (in very short form): A Chinese farmer's horse runs away. Neighbors sympathize, but the farmer says, "Maybe good, maybe bad." The horse returns with wild horses. Neighbors congratulate, but the farmer says, "Maybe good, maybe bad." The farmer's son breaks his leg trying to tame a wild horse. Neighbors express sorrow, but the farmer says, "Maybe good, maybe bad." A war breaks out, and soldiers avoid the injured son. Neighbors praise the farmer's wisdom as he repeats, "Maybe good, maybe bad."

The lesson? Life is unpredictable; what appears good or bad initially may *by chance* lead to unexpected outcomes that are in the end more favorable. Keep an open mind to the chances that may come next: If you are focusing on the bad of each situation you will leave a much smaller gap for the good to find its way in.

Relating the idea of chance to creating things: there is no thing you may create that will make you fulfilled forever, there is also no such thing to me as a bad creation, at least we cannot know that something is bad completely as it may lead us to somewhere "good" later on. Sure maybe you created something only to get rid of it, but that does not mean it can't be fuel for chance in your path ahead.

A very real example of this is creating things that aren't meant to last: The chef makes food even though they know it's going to be "destroyed" in a sense. The plating is perfected even though it's about to be demolished, the wedding cake extravagantly molded even though it's time is ticking, the ice sculpture hand crafted only to melt away a few hours after it's big reveal.

In this sense we know what comes next, the creator knows what's going to happen: but the creator creates the thing anyways, because by chance someone may enjoy what they have created. And by chance it may make them feel fulfilled in hearing such praise, or by chance they find themselves lost in creating itself and they did not think about the outcome really, they just wanted to take part in the process of creating something.

In general: The chances of "good things" or anything happening expand when you are creating things. Your ability to keep creating things is enhanced by looking at each event as not good or bad, but a new chance.

Each thing we create may fuel our lives on different levels, by the chance of our memories coming back to visit us or by the chance that someone remembers what we once created. All of it, in the end, is unknown. Unknown at least until we experience the chance coming to us... so it seems the only way to proceed is to make some noise, to create some things, and see how chance favors us.

// And oh! What fun it is, to approach such a chance with excitement. For we do not know what is to come: the world may be rotting, and the world may be flourishing, both can be true at the same time. We can enjoy either inquiry, we can be curious about what we can make of each moment. This is a much more riveting experience: to allow a larger entry way for the chance of goodness to come in and find us.

seventeen.

Starting over

When you are creating things, a lot of the time you will find yourself at a peak of resistance: especially if something is rather difficult. This peak constitutes a choice between two options. The first option being to keep going until you get past this resistance, and ultimately find yourself at the same crossroads in due time. The second option is to start over, to toss in the towel on something that isn't working, so you can create something that does.

Starting over is a less common option, and a lot of the time you really do just need to keep going through resistance because progress, or growth is equal to struggle. Resistance is almost always progress in some way, but it may be a sign to start over too (which could be quite progressive). Learning to know when to quit is a powerful thing, if you find your curiosity is fading or looking somewhere else that is usually a slight indicator that it may be time to start over. *// But not always. You'll have to trial and error with this for yourself, sorry: your truth may be different than mine.*

Start over on what? Well that depends on you. In many cases I have created things that were at first in line with my curiosity, sometimes I become more curious about something else in relation to what I'm doing than the thing I'm doing itself. So I start over on my knowledge gaps. I dive into what I don't know and am curious about, I let myself be guided by this sense. This has worked for me quite well to know when I should try something new, but it's also missing a logical side. For example: I created something that took me three years to create, then my curiosity switched gears. I found that my old creation was not helping me anymore but rather it was pulling me back. So taking all of the many things I learned from my old creation I started with a blank canvas.

Much like when an artist learns to paint, they don't reuse the same canvas every time to preserve their past work, they grab a new canvas and put the other one aside, they use their past learnings to create new pieces of work and they continue in this process until their hands grow tired of doing so or until they croak. Starting over is not as blank of a canvas as it seems. If you are starting over on creating something then you have some backlog of imagination and information. You can use this to create something better than before. It may feel painful to "start from scratch" – no one wants to lose progress. Even so, no one is ever really starting over, they are just backtracking so they can push ahead further.

Take this image I drew for example: (next page)

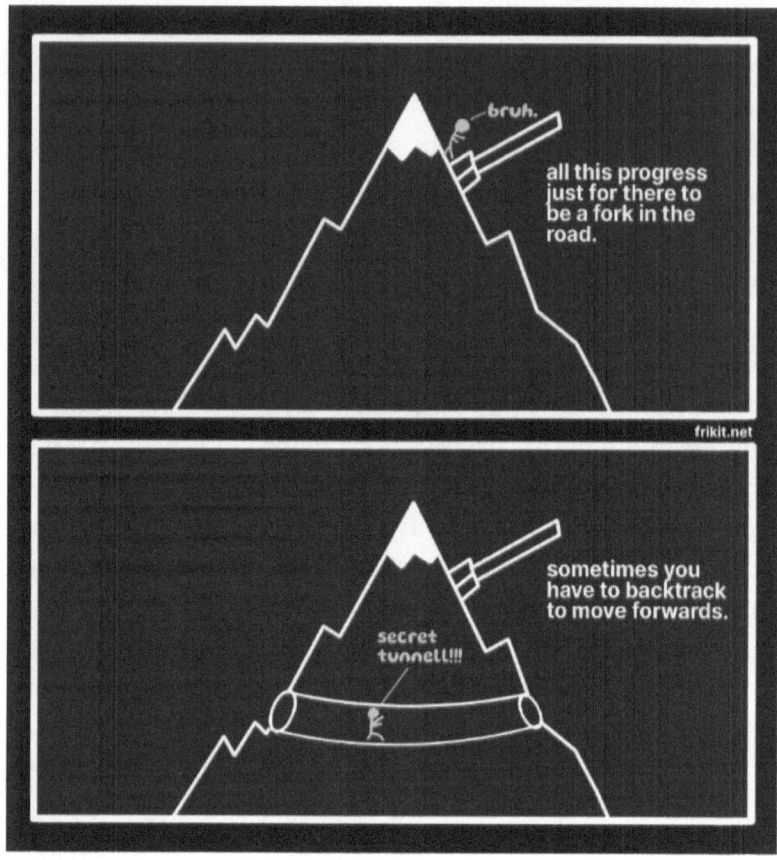

sometimes you really do just have to start over, or go backwards: so you can reach a further destination on your absolutely unique path.

A large part of starting over is accepting the fact that you can't move forwards while looking back. This is to say: you are either going forwards, or you're going backwards. If you are going backwards, make sure it's so you can soon go forwards again.

eighteen.

Everyone is winging it

No one really knows what they're doing. Out of the billions of humans that exist, I don't believe any one of them has it "all figured out". In addition to no one having it all figured out, I would go as far to say that every single human is in some grandeur capacity: just winging it.

Each and every one of us can make plans, we can craft wonderful visions, we can create things not yet imagined, and we can even out perform extraordinarily bad odds… but this pesky thing remains as a thorn in our side: the unknown. Ultimately the "unknown" is the idea that we have no way of knowing what we do not know, we can only really know the startling reality that we know very little in the grand scheme of things.

Einstein didn't know what he would invent. You could reasonably say he was winging it when it came to the outcomes of his many experiments. This is a great example in the context of creating things especially.

You will never know which failure adds the final piece to the puzzle, the one that connects your dots of accumulated knowledge all together... So the only logical approach to do something great with your life is to get up and try: to wing it.

I wasn't best friends with Einstein but I can also tell you this about him: he lived his life and over time he built routines and rituals that suited him best. If you ponder this for a moment you may also realize that this applies to just about anyone on planet earth. We all know very well that each and every one of us is just winging it. We just don't like to think about it too much. Your way of life: to try some stuff and then to try some more stuff as you go to see what works best for you. Well, it's the same approach for life as all of the greats used who came before you. The ones who created the bedrock of civilization we stand on top of today... they too were simply "just winging it" in the most rudimentary sense, using the known things of their time.

To wing it is to try without knowing for certain if it will work. Today there are infinitely more unknowns than there are knowns: so our only choice is to wing it, this is how we gain more data to work with, so we can better wing it next time.

This could be a scary thought to think about for you, or an exciting one. The scary part is that in accepting that everyone is just winging it, you also accept that there is no human messiah that has all the answers. This means that your parents, your grandparents, the richest people on earth: they are all just people who have figured some stuff out and are basing their future decisions on what they have come to know through winging it. They are still winging it as we speak, and just like you: they can't stop even if they wanted to.

It may be scary to think about how everyone is just going with the flow of what they have come to know, but it's also equally exciting. It's exciting to know that everyone is just winging it. If everyone is winging it then it also means that you aren't the only one who is absolutely lost at times. It's exciting to know that you aren't the only lost buffoon around, that there are many others who also have no idea where life will lead them in the end, or even next. Everyone has multiple points in their existence where they had no clue what to do, so what do you do and what's the only option to do? Why to wing it of course! To try something, anything at all: or to do nothing as a form of doing something; even if just to see what happens from inaction.

No matter how the cards play out, bluff about it all you want, you were winging it, as are we all. – because you can't possibly know, all of which you don't know.

nineteen.

Play comes before work?

"Do what feels like play to you, but looks like work to others" - Naval Ravikant

In this chapter I want to cover how we can go about turning work into something that feels like play. Afterall, play is not just for children, it's for everyone (especially the working human).

"All work and no play makes Jack a dull boy" - James Howell's Proverbs (1659)

You may look at this quote and think about how obvious it is, of course no one should just be working all the time: that would be no fun at all! I look at it in that way too, but I also see a third side to this coin of work: The third side being the edge of the coin that says: work can feel like play, if you find the work that feels playful to you.

Finding such work however is a mysterious mountain. A mountain that can't be climbed with brute force, but rather must be climbed by curiosity. Before we think about climbing such a mountain though you might want to know more about why you would want to find work that feels like play to you, so let's cover that first, then I'll tell you how to go about finding such "work".

Why do you want to play at work?

The goal about finding work that feels like play is not to always be playful, but to feel like you're at play more often than you feel like you're working. // *Work is still a valuable thing to do, no matter how it feels. Humans can inherit a lot of fulfillment from partaking in any kind of work.*

The quote I opened this chapter with: *"Do what feels like play to you, but looks like work to others"* is worded very deliberately.

*"what **feels** like play to you"* means that you are searching in yourself for what is the truth. *"**play**"* meaning it's something fun (to you). *"but **looks**"* because the outside person doesn't have the feel of fun that you do for the task at hand. *"like **work** to them"* means there are people who get paid or are willing to pay someone to do whatever it is you feel is play.

This idea is not suggesting we should work less, on the contrary: it's advocating we find work that feels like play so we can "work" more. So that we can add more to the world, by means of our form of play: which most of the time works out to be us creating or doing things in line with our genuine curiosities.

Why would you want to work more? Well because it's fun to work when it doesn't feel like work. It's fun to work when it feels like play. This is the main feedback loop for this idea.

The secondary and more fruitful feedback loop is that we can use this version of work to quench our curiosity and gain a ton more fulfillment in our lives. The type of

fulfillment gained from being in one's craft (or playful work) is irreplaceable by any means of free time.
//Although life would be no fun in the grand scheme of things if it was just work, even if it was a form of play. Find what matters to you! And find your own balance. This is all really one big adventure to figure out, you likely have the answers to your problems already, locked away in your heart. Work and play are not all the buckets of life, there is also love, friends, family, and much else to help fulfill one's soul.

How do you find work that feels like play?

This is the simplest, but far from the easiest part: You can find work that feels like play to you by **one:** trying lots of things. And by **two:** following your genuine curiosities.

This process may take a lot of time, heck, I'm not still sure if your work can *always* feel like play. Trying to find work that even *most of the time* feels like play, this is a wonderful thing.

For me I've found that many people see what I'm doing for fun (writing, making videos, building stuff) as work. To me however, most of the time, this feels like play. The things I would be happy spending any day of the week doing in a room by myself, these things happen to look like work to others, but feel like play to me.

Your version of this may be very different. For example: There are many people who work 10 hours a day to crochet a sweater together. This seems like a lot of work to me, but to them it just feels like they are playing about. I deem it as work as I find it as something arduous for myself and also because it's something that I could see myself paying someone else to do so I don't have to.

To me, finding your playful work, which may also be defined as "your craft", is a journey for all of life. It does not end when you find the "one thing" because there are likely to be more things you will find that give you this feeling or add to your existing body of "work".

"But..."

A lot of counterarguments to doing work that feels like play is that we need to do hard things in life, or that humans need to work! to sweat! to endure pain!

I agree, I think a life of constant comfort is no good: challenges provide meaning to our existence.

But... doing work that feels like play is not jumping around these things, it is still very much about diving headfirst into the challenges ahead. This time around however, the person facing challenges with an aptitude for the work, because it feels like fun, comes out on top: pretty much every single time.

Play in the sense of work nurtures optimism, and nowadays it makes a lot more sense to be overly optimistic than it does to be a reasonable pessimist. There is no lion nearby coming to eat you in your air-conditioned home, so why be pessimistic enough to think that the world will eat you up at each and every turn? Why not try to have a little fun?

The person who is overly optimistic is the person who dares to try what is thought to be a sure-fire failure. Sometimes it very well does fail, the persistent was right, wow, hip hip hurray to failing! But this is not how the story goes... there is no applause for being a correct pessimist. There is also no progress being made in constantly thinking about how something "isn't going to work". Flipping the switch for thinking about how something can work is much more productive and progressive, and this is where *fun* drives us towards. To make progress even when the odds are against us, even when the pessimists say *"it just won't work"*. The optimist tries anyways, for what's the worst that could happen? Especially if the challenge is one that feels like play.

// afterword addition: I am attempting to create an app that helps people find this sort of play. I may fail at doing so, but you can check it out @ curiosityquench.com. // edit of this edit while editing 2nd time around: this is a hard endeavor, still trying, it's been fun :)

twenty.

Create every single day

Something that I've noticed to be a prevailing feature of people who make a lot of progress in life, or enjoy life from the day to day: they are in a consistent cycle of creation.

At the end of each night when you are in bed, can you think of something that you created today? Something you found fun or worthwhile? It would be just grand for your answer to be a consistent yes: but I feel the more common answer on a day to day basis is a no.

You can go about your life as you are now, I'm not saying you have to create something today. I'm only suggesting that you could very well choose to if you wanted to.

"Every single day" is a big part of this equation, that's because as most of us have heard "consistency is key". It's also because it turns out to be quite difficult to **not** find some fulfillment, fun, or lessons when you create something every, single, day. Make some noise, all sorts of paths will open up!

Even without wanting to be a vessel for progress or improvement I think most of us can agree that fulfillment, a sense of purpose, or meaning, are all things we wouldn't mind more of. Whether it's for the purpose of finding your interests, exploring your curiosity, or doing hard things to build a better reputation with yourself: creating things helps us see not only who we are, but who we can become.

To create everyday is a way of discovering what the world has to offer for you and what you have to offer to the world, bit by bit, and of course: day by day. Over time this can indefinitely add to the level of fulfillment we feel and the sense of purpose we have.

To create everyday doesn't mean you can't scroll on social media, or you have to follow a strict protocol: rather this is my way of focusing on what I want to see more of. I want to see more creations in the world, and especially from the people who think they have little to offer or gain from creating. For I myself have found that any day I create things, life unfolds in much more cinematic and enjoyable ways. I would love for others to not only experience this too, but for them to share with me and the world their creations. In totality, adding more cool shit to explore while we live and for the future onset of humans to dive into.

"Once you start doing something every single day: you can bring something into your life that was once a hard thing and now it comes as natural to you as brushing your teeth. - this is not applicable to all things, but only the things you're genuinely curious or interested about." - me (jack friks)

twenty-one. *(do something for me)*

Trying more stuff

Every single day we wake up and make a choice: do we get out of bed? Or do we lay in bed a while longer? This is not the only choice we make in our day, there are thousands of micro and macro choices that happen each and every day.

Of these many choices there are also many chances to take action, to try something new, or to explore inside oneself. Every time you open up social media it's a choice; likely to avoid your own thoughts or unease of boredom. These moments are all proponents of what *could have been*, time that you *could have* spent trying to explore yourself.

Every day you have a choice to do something hard, something worthwhile, or something that will benefit the future version of yourself. You have that choice today, you'll have it again tomorrow.

Of all the choices you can make, I think one of the best to make every day is to try something new, or explore what you like. There are millions, maybe even billions of people who wake up and go about their day with no thoughts as to what else they could do with their extra time, where they could be focusing their mindless hours on social media. They think nothing of how they could spend such time exploring new things, learning about hobbies, crafts, interests that they have which are buried under the frostline of their subconscious scrolling.

If you already have a craft, or a passion project, then you could very well ignore this: but chances are there's something to be discovered in you 'trying more stuff', if you're reading this book.

Trying more stuff leads you to places you probably want to go but didn't yet know. This is because you can't think your way to experience, just like you walk your way across the ocean. Trying stuff is the ideal behind gaining your own experience, your own say in the matter of what you actually enjoy, or don't enjoy.

Honestly I'm not sure you'll be able to know what your "thing" is right away when trying it, and it's likely we all have more than a few things we really can get excited about or find ourselves lost in. The thing about trying more things is that it opens our entire lives scope up. The more we know about ourselves the more potential *optimal* pathways open up to us; our choices for a healthy, happy, enjoyable life become much less finite the more we do and try stuff.

If you're wondering how you should go about trying more stuff, I think it's quite simple. Find something that sparks your interest, maybe it's chess, maybe it's poker, maybe it's crocheting. Find something that you are inherently intrigued by when you look at it... and instead of looking into all the nitty gritty details of the task: just start doing it. Try it out! If it's gardening that piques your interest then go buy a miniature pot, some soil, and a seed that you can grow in your garden or house. Suddenly you're prompted to go look up "What seeds can I grow indoors?" or "What plant should I grow first?"... by focusing on just trying some stuff in relation to gardening you're instantly miles ahead of when you were just thinking "But is this fun? How does this benefit me in the long run? Will this be worth my time?" - You can get an accurate idea much quicker on the answer to these questions as you actually try things. Maybe you discover gardening is hard, or maybe it's not so hard but you are just bored of it. Well now you can try something else. Maybe you'll come back to gardening one day too, who knows.

Trying trials

I myself have been very interested in making videos on the internet. I took up this interest years ago and it led me to where I am today. To write! I love writing now a whole lot too, but when I first started making videos, I didn't so much. To me the task of writing was a chore, it was little fun, and mostly work.

After making 1000+ videos over time, pondering through my thoughts talking to a camera I came to a realization that writing is my preferred medium of thinking. It helps me get out of my brain what I really need to say, and how I can best say it. In realizing this I came to realize I actually love writing. It's something I tried out many years ago and pushed aside, mostly because I was trying other things, looking for my golden egg... when the real golden egg was right under my nose all along.

Trying more stuff is not a search for the golden egg or the thing that you absolutely can't stop thinking about. It's more so about building up a list of things you have experienced, so that you can guide yourself better or come to more optimal conclusions for your own life.

Note: Some things take a lot of time to *try*, you can speed up the time required to come full circle by increasing the variable that is your level of focus. The more focus you give an interest, the hastier it gets cracked open for what it really is (to you). It took me years to come full circle to realize I enjoyed writing as much as I did: this is because my focus was scattered between things that didn't actually matter.

Where do you focus? *Focus on what actually matters to you*; **Focus on what you want to see more of.**

Trying more stuff is not a guaranteed way to become great at something, but it is a way of increasing chance. The chance that you'll come to the realization of what matters most to you, where you should be putting your focus, and what you should be doing with your time. Trying more stuff is really just another way of saying "gain more experience".

Now, stop reading this book, go try some stuff (or go to sleep and try some stuff tomorrow).

Currently, my favorite way to try more stuff is to go about writing in different ways, reading different types of books, and creating different things (I'm building an app as I write this book to help people find new interests and take action on them daily, I'm also trying to destroy death scrolling addictions simultaneously).

twenty-two.

Something I wish someone would have told me earlier but I'm kinda glad they didn't

For a lot of my life I grew up confused as to where I was going. This isn't to say that I had no idea about some of the things I desired for my future, but rather I had a feeling that there was something astray with the world view I had inherited from my parents.

It took me until I was around 21 when something autonomous clicked in my brain, for the first time I realized that my parents were only human like me. At this time in my life I realized a few distinct things: [*Everyone is winging it*], [*Your life really is **your** life, you can choose how you live it*], [*There is no shame in getting excited that you're on your own adventure*], and finally, the thing I wish someone told me earlier, but I'm kinda glad they didn't: [*Suppressing your unique sovereignty (where you want to go, who you want to be, what type of life you* want to **create**) is a losing game not only for you, but those around you too. And yes, even for those who you really don't want to upset with your acts of sovereignty]

The reason I'm glad no one told me about my own sovereignty being a very important thing is because ironically this lesson is best found in an autonomous fashion.

If someone were to tell me when I was sixteen that it's okay to have my own free will, that I should go after who I want to be, where I want to go, and what I want to create, even if others thought it was silly... Well I probably wouldn't be here, I wouldn't be who I am today; and I really like where + who I am today.

// *I also probably wouldn't have listened to such sage wisdom when I was sixteen, or taken it to heart, so there's that too.*

Next time you wish you had done something differently, or you find yourself wishing you knew something sooner: also think about how much it would alter who you are and what you want to be now: at some point you're going to reach the place where you don't want to know more things sooner, you'll just be happy to know them at all when you come to know them. This is likely the day you not only realize your love for yourself, and how valuable it is to love oneself, but also this is the day you realize that you had it right all along, in deep down knowing you needed to try things yourself, to make your own decisions, as well as make your own mistakes.

All along the world was asking you only to do one thing: to create your own adventure, to make your life your own.

This chapter doesn't necessarily only pertain to how you were built to create things, but it does tell you that life is very much about creating your own path.

The reason I believe creating things to be so important is not just because you can end up making something for others to use or enjoy, and it's not only because it feels good to create things, rather: it's very important to create things because you are the creator in charge of your own life. And the more you come to create things, to choose to create things frequently, the more you realize your own autonomy in the world, your own sovereignty, and the more curious you become about what adventure you can plunder into next. Creating things is a development of thoughts, and adventure: creating things is the expression of your own autonomy, and that is why creating things is important. To help you believe in yourself, even if just a little bit more. And to help you go on your own adventure, excited about what is to come next whatever it may be.

twenty-three.

A friendly pep talk

I'm going to write as if you are my close friend who I want to see find more of the joy in life and more of the joy in creating things: feel free to skip this chapter if you don't need a pep talk.

My dear friend,

I hope you're doing well, it's been awhile since we last spoke. Since I haven't heard from you in quite a while I figured I'd send out a reminder to you in case you've forgotten some of the important things to *remember* in trying times. Not that I think you're in trying times, but you know... couldn't hurt?

First off I want you to know that I love you, and I can love you because I've taken the time to love myself first. You don't need to tell me you love me back. If you don't mean it, I have enough love: you can borrow some of it, it's no trouble. If I am in need of love I shall ask for some, we can work together you know?

Regardless, I just wanted to let you know what's on my mind, and share with you some of the joy I've been able to find in life lately (maybe you can find some joy in my joy too). First off, I've been making things, creating them if you will. Actually, I'll spill the beans with you, I'm writing a book! What a fantastic experience it is. To be able to put my thoughts onto a page and think about them as words I've put into the world, to be able to rearrange my own thoughts as I think them, it's an ever evolving and equally splendid process. It's also kind of like I'm moving my feet under my own command, much different than if I had to make something of myself for my creations, I'm just having a blast in the process.

Enough about me though... I'm writing this for you, my dear friend. I've come to ask you some questions today, or rather: I've come to give you some questions today. Questions for you to ask yourself. You don't have to answer all of them, but man, some of these questions had my mind turning over, not in a grave, but rather onto a new page of life: a page with a giant map ready for adventure.

Welp, here are the questions:

Enjoy :)
- What do I want out of life? How can I get more of it?

_____ *- What is something I'm curious about?*

*- How can I **create** around my curiosities? (document, experiment, share, collaborate, expand?)*

- *Where am I going now? How does it differ from where I want to go?*

_____
_____
_____
_____
_____

Do I love myself? Why? Why not?

_____
_____
_____
_____
_____

Again: **you don't need to answer all of these questions**. *Many of these questions may not have direct answers anyhow. They may instead prompt more questions inside of you naturally... That's the fun part about asking questions.*

Finally, here's something I wrote about life in that may help you through any trying times, please come back to this if you ever find yourself being overly hard on yourself:

"Perhaps a large part of this masquerade we call life is that we have no idea how far we can take ourselves and it scares the bejeebies out of us. To think that we could be a pawn freely promoting itself at the end of the board, but end up stuck on the second line of life. From this point of view you're living up to something, but in reality we've set up a false hierarchy. We need not to be continuously promoting ourselves. More so: we need to be continuously loving ourselves enough to fight the battle we find worthwhile." – me (your friend)

It's funny how life works you know: we are born, we live, we die... that's the gist of it, but somewhere in the middle there are some magical moments, moments only we can hold onto. How something made us feel, how we did something hard, or worthwhile (usually both), or how we explored our own thoughts and discovered a hidden piece of knowledge. Life is full of these magical moments. So the next time you're thinking of how you haven't had a magical moment in a long while, take note that it usually means one is close around the bend, and it's coming your way.

And life really is magical y'know, to think we're even here right now, existing, it's a wild thing, isn't it?

Write me a letter back and tell me how you're doing, what's on your mind? What's got you down, or what's got you up! Tell me all about it.

*With love,
your friend,
jack* ♠

– Take some time to reflect on the questions I asked in this letter, and if you are so inclined: journal up a draft of your response to this, as a friend.

You can send it to me at **jack@frikit.net**, you can tweet it at me on twitter @jackfriks, or you can simply keep it to yourself. Regardless I feel that you will benefit a good amount if you're to take up this challenge, even if only for 5 minutes. - Only do so if it interests you though, otherwise, carry on with paying attention to where your attention leads you next. Do whatever compels you.

twenty-four.

Learning without pressure to perform and the ghost of dread

When I was in college I learned a good amount of things about my chosen field (computer programming). However, I dropped out of college in my final year. I still got a diploma for my first 2 years of school, as opposed to an "advanced diploma", but the reality I've come to realize is that school is not a great place to learn things you're genuinely interested in, or curious about. Or at the very least in my experience alone: school did not grow my curiosity but instead suppressed it.

I've only come to realize recently that this is the case, 3 years after I dropped out from college. The moment I realized this is when I decided I needed and wanted to learn python (a computer programming language). My curiosity led me to this point, to learn so I could make an application I wanted to exist in the world but did not yet. When I started to learn python through some YouTube videos I started to feel the same sense of wonder and curiosity I did in my first days of college… yes *days*, not *weeks*. My curiosity was quickly put to rest in college and would only come back to say hello on sparse occurrences. However, when I was learning more or less the same type of things I learned in college, this time from a YouTube video I sought out on my own, I ended up remaining curious for many days, I wanted to keep learning! More important than my desire to continue learning, I was finding joy in learning, it was fun: my curiosity only grew in this time.

Did everything end up exactly as I'd hoped when I set out to learn more coding? No, of course not. But something that happened this time around that didn't happen in college is that my curiosity didn't get crushed or squished. I didn't have to think about how "employable" each of my curiosities were, I could just learn to learn, because I wanted to learn. I didn't need to factor how one lesson to the next would help me land a big comfy job at some top company. The only thing I had to think about was what I wanted to learn, and then I could spend time enjoying my time learning it. This is how I believe a [good] learning experience should look like.

Now, on the note of "the ghost of dread" as titled above, I want to talk about teaching. In a lot of the classes I took the teachers lacked their own curiosity for their work, and overall they lacked a genuine interest to teach it. Sure, they knew their stuff, they could land a job doing what they taught (If it were still applicable: colleges typically, or at least mine, was about 4-8 years behind on curriculum compared to the real working world's preferred programming languages and best technology practices).

In general the teachers who did have a spark of interest or a curiosity to teach made learning a worthwhile and enjoyable experience. Sadly these professors were far and few between. The ghost of dread came along with most of the teachers in my path, the dread of being there, having to teach, it wasn't hard to tell the dread was there; for most of the teachers had little interest to show their own interest in what they were teaching. I can't entirely blame them, some of the stuff is boring, outdated, and not a requirement if they were to drag us into the real world. It's hard to be excited about things you believe not to be entirely important, you understand don't you, fellow human?

On top of this, I want to remind you about the notion that we are all completely unique individuals with our own unique curiosities. Sure a curriculum may be good to help student X get a job, or explore certain parts of their curiosity, but the curriculum is not enough to quench each and every student's curiosities, it's just not possible. Nor is it fair to expect the same curriculum to answer all your questions or all of your problems. In a lot of common cases the main point of college is to give you the knowledge you need to get a job. This is fine. I have no ill will against my college experience; especially because I didn't go into debt to get this education… but in the eyes of creation, in the way of following one's genuine curiosities: the internet, and books all around will quench your thirst much more appropriately.

You will be able to learn about what you are genuinely curious about in a ridiculously more enjoyable way if you are left to your own devices to learn what you really want to learn. In contrast to learning about how you can best be suited to land a job. Different approaches to learning for different outcomes is all.

Learning without: [the dread of teachers who don't want to teach] + [the feeling that everything is leading up to a pressurized chamber of tests, quizzes, exams, presentations and resume building] this is learning on your own free will, with your own autonomy of curiosity, and this is where the best learning comes from, this is where people learn without thinking about learning. This is where it is second nature to improve your brain's understanding about whatever it may be you are curious about. This is the space in-between thoughts that great and joyous things are created. This is where work feels like play and action happens without a thought. Resistance will still occur no doubt, but it will be much different.

twenty-five.

Information overload

The most valuable information is not always the most scarce, it's just boring. So many people won't bother to look where it lies. Today, with the internet, it wouldn't be an understatement to say that the volume of information we have available to us is often more of a hindrance than it is a helping hand.

Valuable information is free, it's abundant. But the thing about this is that there is so much information being created, compiled and put out there on a minute by minute basis that one could not consume all the information on the internet in their lifetime. Even if it was only the last few hours of newly added information.

According to the latest estimates (in 2023), 328.77 million terabytes of data are created every day. That's about 2.5 billion iPhone worth of data put onto the web every day.

$$\text{Number of iPhones} = \frac{328{,}770{,}000{,}000 \text{ GB}}{128 \text{ GB}}$$

$$\text{Number of iPhones} \approx 2{,}567{,}578{,}125$$

Now, I know using iPhone is probably not the best measure for efficient storage, really though I needed to give you some frame of reference for how ridiculous our situation is in terms of information available to us.

Majority of the data is also in video format, which takes a good amount of time longer to consume than it would to read.

With this in mind, can you believe a book is only $10?

In order for a book to be made, especially one with specific knowledge on a subject, the author has to sort through an endless pile of information, implement it to see if it's any good, do this for many years, and then write it down into words you can understand. Sure these are only a few simple processes... but to get the same information in the sea of information out there, well it may take more time than you can spare. You may never get to know what you need to know if you were left to your own curation devices.

Not only is there too much data to curate and learn from, but in order to learn well you would also have to take some action on all the information you are consuming; which would be endless, so you'd never be able to learn much at all if you were trying to curate the storm of data all by yourself. This is where books come to play a large part in curating useful information. And they are only like ten dollars, isn't that a wild thing?

For ten dollars you get a look into someone's body of work, research, and many of their experiences. You can learn the lessons that took them years to figure out, in a few days, and apply them in a fraction of time (Yes you do have to take action on advice for it to be useful, hint: *use*-full, meaning it is *used*). Valuable information has been lived through and expressed into words just for you to read. Not all books are about valuable information of course, but the majority of non-fiction books fall under this premise. Years of someone's life: put into words in a book, someone else's human experience captured in a medium of words for you to consume and equip yourself with.

Valuable information is not scarce, it's just hard to compile efficiently in a sea of data. Books compile data and lived *experience* very well, and all for a very modest price tag.

Valuable information is freely available all around us, but to find it is like a needle in a haystack. Not only that: but when we come across the needle by complete accident: we throw it back in the haystack because it's often too simple or boring of an answer, we need not bother, we must keep looking for the *magical* solution, the *shortcut*. The "shortcut" is usually the longest path to real fulfillment in the end, in case you were wondering.

There's a weird phenomenon about information, we have so much of it available to us, but we fail to use really any part of it effectively to better ourselves. It's almost as if we enjoy our own misery in a lot of ways, like we don't want to know the answer because we do not like the answer. Maybe we believe there is a better answer around the corner, so we wait our entire lives for it to come, but it never does. So the simple answer to get anything done, or put any information into action to see if it's valuable is just to try, perhaps fail, and try again until you decipher the valuable from the invaluable. In an age of information overload the best way to sort through the endlessly growing heap of hay and find a teeny tiny needle is to take action, any action at all. To "just do it". To create some things and learn from what goes wrong. If we are ever going to get anywhere it starts with taking the first steps.

// I may need to write another chapter on the art of inaction or finding out the best action is to do nothing, but I haven't quite figured these scenarios out myself. So I'll leave you with the motivation that you should probably do more things, as opposed to less. For most people I think this is a better scenario: and if it isn't you'll learn that quickly enough with your own actions.

Comparing my book to other more researched or experienced authors, my book is an odd scramble of thoughts. But books also offer another great form of consumption and that is concentrated attention and belief building. Throughout my book someone can come along with me for my ride and see life through a new lens they may not have acquired yet, that in itself is invaluable (I think, *slight bias*), and books offer this, but articles or videos don't really, or at least not nearly as much. Books have staying power because there is so much to sort through and it's all in one place to be found. It's not in a scattered sea of data like most information on the internet, but rather in a tidy map of concentrated adventure.

With my book's points, my hope is that you will feel inspired to create something of your own, create said thing(s) and live a better life for it... do I know if that will happen? No I don't, how could I? But here I am trying regardless, to see what happens, to give it a go anyhow.

All we can do to see what happens is to first try.

twenty-six.

The rules are made up and no one cares

This is a good thing... At the end of the day there is no rule on planet earth (other than the natural laws of nature) that hasn't been entirely made up by someone just like you: i.e. a human being

Note to self and the reader: Maybe these aren't even so much as only "rules" I'll be referring to, but ways of doing or being, as a comment from someone on the internet phrased: "I prefer to see life "on Earth" in terms knowing/ discovering / implementing, as Lao Tzu would call things, The Way. Don't call them rules. Look for "The Way" to do things."

So a lot of rules are not so much rules, but a lack of knowing why something is or isn't a certain way(these are important things to figure out!). You will likely find it helpful to find the right way for you, or the right set of human principles for you to follow on your unique path. Perhaps phrasing this as "rules" is my wrong way of doing, I'm not entirely sure just yet, there is something there but a puzzle is missing in my brain. So, here is what I have to say about the rules (in the essence of finding your own way about life).

The weird part about the rules is not only that they are entirely fabricated out of thought and created by a brain no much more developed than yours... the weirdest part is that they are often followed blindly, with no thought or self-sovereignty whatsoever. The rules have janked up our autonomous selves, and right now I want to try and help you see the humor of it all.

Think about this: April 1st is the day that you can pull practical pranks and jokes on all of your friends without repercussions. This is known as April fools, it's a rule that the 1st day of April is nationally a pranking day. What's funny about this rule is that we have all blindly accepted it since we were born, but have you ever wondered where April fools came from? Do you know? Well... the truth is, no one *really* knows why April fools is April fools. Some people have guesses, or hunches about its origin, but no one really knows. This is two parts humorous because on the 1st part: it's about April fools. And on the second part it's funny because even though we have no idea why, we still prank all of our friends on this day every year.

Children do a great job of being curious enough to ask questions like "Why is April fools a thing?", or "Why is April fools on April 1st?": This is interesting to note. April fools is just one small example, an innocent, noncontroversial example.

There are a million more examples of rules we have embraced without thought that are not so fun to think about. The rules of higher minimum employee wages, the rules against marriage with the same sex, the rules against women voting, all of these have been tried against because they are clear violations of our human rights to exist as we wish, so long as we are not harming others in the process.

In this manner of despicable rules that have plenty of people up in arms, there are also shadow rules which have drastic effects on our daily lives. Shadow rules is a coin I'm phrasing now, which basically means that there is a rule that follows you around in your brain that you don't question, it's just a rule that's there: like your shadow, you wouldn't tell it to bug off, because you believe that there's no other way about it.

A shadow rule, which is made up by a fellow human, like all the other rules: is something that you have likely been made to think is a rule even though it's not. A rule in which you aren't even aware you have set up for yourself. Take something like the rule "I can't move out of my mom's basement until X happens" - This is a rule I once set for myself, I thought it was true because I didn't have copious amounts of money laying around to pay for more expensive rent, but the truth is, it's not true at all. It's a rule I had come to in my head that was just not so, as most of the rules we set for ourselves: they need evaluation and re-evaluation to fit into our ever changing and one of a kind world view.

A shadow rule may also look like a set of family guidelines, or outside opinions for how *you* should live *your* life. Many parents tell their kids to go to college **or else**. There is instantly a rule put into the child's brain *"It's college or it's the big scary outside world so I must go to college"* Whether or not any decision is a good one is not the point here. The point is that outside voices are often a setter of rules for someone else's life, and this is just wrong on many levels (not all, but many), so I hope I can make you aware of this if you weren't already: For many parts of life where you think you only have one option, one path, **you can** *play by your own rules. You can create a new set of game rules for the game that's **your** life.*

When it comes to many of the normal rules of life like don't die, don't do something criminal, don't steal what's not yours, don't drink someone else's pee, wash your hands to clean them... these are not the rules I'm speaking of when it comes to you making your own playbook. So, with that in mind: let's talk about some more of the uncomfy aspects of what we can and cannot do as humans in the 21st century.

The second part of the title above is "no one cares", what I mean by this is: everyone is paying attention to themselves far more than they are paying attention to you. Example: The pretty girl you are worried about seeing you as a fool is too busy trying to hide her pig snort when she laughs to think of your goofy mistake(s).

Even if you make a mistake or fail in public, you may think all these people are thinking bad thoughts about you when in reality, they are not, and even if they were: it wouldn't change your reality anyhow. No one cares more about you than they do themselves (with an exception for good parents).

Let's now mix two trains of thought: the "rules" and the fact that no one really cares about what you do (they are too busy worrying about themselves). Let's say you could spend all your life doing what you love and only that, no one will physically stop you, you may think "well I can't do that because then..." because then you'll be lacking something else you want? Probably! Now the choice is: what do you want more than the other. The most common blockade to this path of life is feeling uncomfortable. Uncomfortable that you have little money, or that your parents are not proud of you. Uncomfortable with not fitting in to how the rest of the world operates. This is common for anyone doing something different. I'm not suggesting here that you drop your current life and go move to the mountains to paint. Instead, I'm suggesting that there are active possibilities we all subconsciously weigh in our heads for what our life could be.

You can move to the mountains, there is no rule against it other than your own rules or the ones imposed on you by others: knowing this is freeing, and now you can realize you have the choice for many options you may have *ruled* out all together.

"You are the chief storyteller of your own life, and as the Monarch of your life, you get to decide what is meaningful, what is beautiful, what is good, and so on" – Visakan Veerasamy

twenty-seven.

The Creation Megaphone

The internet has enabled witchcraft for the masses. Anyone with an internet connection can now make something and find people to enjoy it. No matter how niche or specific it may be there are thousands of people ready to line up for someone's creation.

This new phenomenon of the internet has created with it a whole new dynamic for the creation process which makes it easier to: create things, learn how to create things, and share your creations with others.

A reason why the internet may be considered witchcraft isn't just because it's held together by invisible signals, but more so because a single person can have an immediate impact and influence over thousands, even **millions** of people.

The click of one button sending out information can lead to twenty-thousand people lining up at a local mall for a burger shop grand opening. A short video of your garden could easily reach hundreds of thousands of people. The internet is a megaphone for anything you create that can be seen by billions of potential eyeballs.

I won't go into the potential downsides that this megaphone brings, as you already probably know how a never ending scroll affects our brains in many ways. Rather, I want to focus on your involvement with using such a megaphone and your participation in creating things/cool shit.

Sharing your vibe, even if no one sees it

I know I said that a simple video could reach millions of people, and that's not a lie at all, but considering you created and posted about something on the internet and no one took notice, no one saw your creation... would the thing that you created still exist? Well of course it would.

Just because no one sees what you are creating doesn't mean it ceases to exist. You will have benefited from being in the process at some point of creation, from being involved with what was in front of you, and you have undoubtedly added one more piece of yourself to the world via creation. Sharing your creations means that you were confident enough that what you have created is worth something, it's a signal to yourself that you value what you are doing. Even if no one sees what you're creating, you've left your mark. Most of the process in creation is invisible, it can't be documented, it can only be felt as you are in such a state.

If you think to someone who has created something worthwhile they had to develop a sense of "I don't care if other people don't see what I'm creating, I'm creating it anyways, because I enjoy creating it" – of course this doesn't apply to every creation of our world, this is better applied to one based in lifelong crafts. Nonetheless, it's useful to note that anyone chasing likes over a creation process is probably in it for reasons not in line with their own being (whether these are the right reasons or the wrong ones I'll let you decide).

Do you need to use a megaphone?

The internet lets us share our creations far and wide, but do we really need to share them at all? This answer is completely up to you, but I would say "it depends" – this is probably the most common answer to a hard question, and it's not much of an answer alone so let's go over what exactly it "depends" on.

First, it depends if you are creating something for the sake of itself. If you are, then no you don't need to amplify your creation on the internet, but if you want to then go right ahead.

Second, it depends if you are trying to make progress on your creations. If you are, then the internet is an effective approach to see the real level of your progress and ask for help to improve (feedback, lack of interest, etc.)

Third, it depends if you can share your creations more locally in the context of real life first, then you may not need external feedback outside of your non-internet feedback

Fourth, it depends if your creations are shareable things to begin with. A lot of creations are less visible or tangible and therefore are harder to really "share": connections, love, families, friendships, management, community, etc.

Finally, it depends if you want to enjoy the process itself and leave it at that, or if you want to amplify it with the internet as your megaphone: either option is fine.

The real lesson here is that the internet is a great tool, we can use it to amplify our creations like a megaphone, or we can leave it by the wayside as we create whatever it is that we are curious about. A tool may not be used by all creators, just as a writer has no use for a hammer to improve their writing, you may not need such a tool for your creations.

As a final note for this chapter, when you are on the internet there is a certain useful approach you may want to consider taking when people tell you how to live your life. This is my approach to those people who have nothing better to do with their life than to tell you how to live yours:

"I've found it's much more beneficial to be a village idiot in the age of the internet than it is to try and appear smart... in a world where everyone wants you to tell you how to live your life, let them: and then go off and do your own thing anyhow." - jack friks. (me)

On top of this, if someone is to say "you are wrong!", it would be better to inquire sincerely or curiously as to why they think that than it would be to disagree. There is a lot to learn from other people, and there are a lot of genuine people out there among the unpleasant people. Finding them will do you well, or at least it has been this way for me when sharing my creations with the world. It's not worth your time to get angry at strangers on the internet, it is *possibly* worth your time to understand why they made you so bothered (only you can know).

twenty-eight.

Time in *the zone,* and *going deep*

Creating things that come from your innate curiosity depends on you, for some period of time, to be in *the zone*. Put differently this is the act of working on something in deep consciousness rather than in shallow. This zone may still be a little unfamiliar to you: that's fine.

You may be able to recall a feeling of extreme focus that once you started a task you could not stop until you were done. No matter what tried to pull you away. Matter of fact, as I write this I'm in this sort of state. I was reading a book, and an idea popped into my head for this chapter, and off I went to jot down my thoughts, without a thought.

You can harness this zone too and in general: add more depth to your life. Not only will you likely enjoy the time you spend in this state, but you'll also reap major rewards in terms of progression. Especially when opposed to any shallow attention you may have been trying to work with. The zone is where focus comes to relax, to settle. This zone is known as depth. Finding depth in your craft and your creations is a crucial part of making something not just meaningful but fulfilling. Another great feature of "going deep" is that you are fully in the now, the present moment, and that is powerful beyond measure for we live in a world that is constantly trying to take us away from this very moment... which turns out to be the only thing we truly have.

How do you get into more depth? I have a few things that have worked for me techniques wise, of which I'll share with you in this Chapter. But I'd also highly suggest picking up the book "Deep Work" by Cal Newport for a deeper dive into depth (a dive that has served me very well). Another great book about the "now" is "The Power of Now" by Eckhart Tolle. *// book recommendation in a book, how fitting, I know.*

The first thing I'll say about the idea of depth is that it works a lot better on goal-oriented things than not. You don't necessarily need depth for all the things you create, but at the same time: it would be silly to not acknowledge all the types of juicy fruit that fully concentrated effort can yield (or just the power of focusing on the current moment as it happens).

Something like playing an instrument comes easy to develop depth for, because what else can you really be doing if you have a tuba on your lap? You can play it or think about how you can play it better.

On the other hand, when 'the work' is boiled down to clicking your fingers on the keyboard or your phone screen (knowledge based work): we have a much different story on our hands.

This chapter may not directly apply to all the creators reading this, but it certainly will be useful for all creators to examine.

To get into a state of "the zone" or depth you'll first have to be void of distractions.

Take away all devices that serve you notifications, set a time limit on your focus, hone in on one task, and spend the entire time either doing that task or staying focused until the task is complete.

If the task is monstrous, then chip away at it in segments by setting mini-goals or something similar. I started getting into the zone for writing my book (the one you are reading now) with twenty-five-minute sessions. I used a Pomodoro timer but usually didn't take any rest because, after ten-fifteen minutes of work, you tend to become so enthralled with the task you won't want to stop. This is because being deep in the zone feels good; not just eating a candy-bar good, but soul-food good.

Being in the zone for me gives me a lightness to my step as the day goes on... I'm not sure why this is, but I enjoy it, nonetheless.

I would say that the above is the most important part of getting into the zone for me, but there is a large precursor to note: I have set large goals and broken them down to daily and session-based tasks. My large goal in this example: To write and self-publish a book (this book), my daily task: write a thousand words, my session task: undistracted focus on writing for twenty-five minutes. Not all things creation-based need this thought out goal process, but a lot of things that will require a large amount of depth benefit from having actionable things to y'know... *act on.*

> *If you are able to focus, and build the muscle of being in the moment with yourself, you will benefit in more ways than just progress or results. Your soul will be well fed and that will carry through the rest of your life in a sense of joy and lightness; if you let it. This is my belief, as woo woo as it may sound.*

twenty-nine.

Boredom is a gift... a good gift.

The uncomfy feeling of boredom is a gift I've come to find. It's a gift to explore yourself, and through this exploration lies a never-ending dance between curiosity and your mind: putting your hands and thoughts to create something interesting, to quench your curiosity, to only end up being curious some more, and then proceeding in repetition.

How's that saying go? Oh well, I better look it up now...

"All of humanity's problems, stem from man's inability to sit quietly in a room alone." - Blaise Pascal

This may seem dramatic in many ways, but if you think on it (which may be slightly uncomfortable to do), it's a real revelation of your mind. Why is it that many of us cannot stand to sit with our own thoughts? Or be bored for any time at all? How can boredom quench curiosity? How can thoughts inspire more thoughts? Or better yet: how does one question lead to the next? (Which may lead to the great answers we seek.)

Well the answers to all of these questions are up in that big noggin of yours. If you only have the capacity to sit quietly and let yourself sort through all the noise already protruding about in your skull: you could probably find some interesting rebuttals to the many questions I just proposed.* // You can also write your answers and thoughts out, this has helped me a lot. Just start writing and see what comes out, don't stop for ten minutes.*

As highlighted in the opening of this chapter, to me boredom is a gift. I used to think being busy was a gift: not having to think about anything other than the work on hand. Sure this can be nice, to work on things that are important to oneself. But what is far superior to being busy is in fact being bored: this is the time you can solve ongoing problems and questions, and if one is always busy but never bored then how can one allow themselves the time to think through where they may be going for the longer haul, the haul of life. Busy-ness is a dangerous state to be locked into for one day you may find yourself bored enough to realize that you have trapped yourself in a cycle of busyness, without knowing how to escape.

Boredom is where the initial thoughts of a meaningful path are laid down, one curiosity after another, in boredom: thoughts create thoughts, ideas create ideas and your life's work may just reveal itself, or not, that's fine too. At the very least, in sitting with boredom you will gain insights into your own mind, which as time goes on will only prove to me more and more valuable. You may also find that after being bored for some time you have newfound inspiration to soon be busy! Busy in a meaningful direction, not just any direction. This is great, to be inspired. When someone is inspired they often create things effortlessly, and things created effortlessly have a certain aura about them. An aura worth soaking up from both the creator, and the consumer.

"To sit with a dog on a hillside on a glorious afternoon is to be back in Eden, where doing nothing was not boring – it was peace." –Milan Kundera

I found the above quote searching for wise words on boredom, this one struck a chord with me: maybe it will for you too. I'll let you think about this quote on your own by reserving my thoughts on it, go fly, fly into your train of thought (If only trains could fly! Well, *at least your thoughts can*).

"You need to let the little things that would ordinarily bore you suddenly thrill you." –Andy Warhol

This quote is interesting too, and this time I'll tell you why. Even though this is quote was said in relativity to being a creative spirit, an artist of sorts (which by now you should know it very well: that we are all creative in spirit) this quote has a ton of meaning in the idea that we need to let ourselves think of being bored as more of an adventure. You can try this now, using the gift of boredom, or lack of interest: try to think about yourself in a way that captures your attention, frame your life as a modern day superhero, or frame your life as if you were exactly where you wanted to be, make whatever frame you have of yourself and make it interesting, think it up so it captures your interest.

...

Well? Did you do it? Have you been enthralled with your own thoughts? Did you get some bit excited? What colour cape were you wearing? Underwear? (if any)

This is where the fun lies in boredom: in imagination! Boredom is also a gift because it lets us foster our imagination, and as our imagination grows, so does the potential of what we deem possible for ourselves... which

I'm sure you can *imagine* how beneficial that is. I hope this chapter bored you (ha ha) (in context).

thirty.

Your animal spirit (life as a movie)

Much of our lives are spent doing things we probably wouldn't choose to be doing if we were proactively considering how it would look in a movie. Take for example that someone was putting your life into a film. In this film now imagine that it was only casted with animals, which animal would you be? Why would you be this animal? Now: What animal would you *prefer* to be? Is it the one that you think represents you, or is there a gap you need to bridge?

All these questions lead to another question which is: What can you do today to be the person you want to see in your life's movie? What can you *focus on* that you want to see more of?

This process may seem wishy washy, *it kind of is...* but the truth is also this: The most cheesy stuff is also usually the most meaningful... or at least this is a truth I've come to believe, maybe I'll put it in my own movie.

Belief is the first step. Do you believe in your own movie? You should.

When I imagine myself as an animal spirit, I would prefer to be the golden retriever of curiosity mixed with a lion of persistence and strength: kind of like a partly goofy, partly curious, but also equally shamanic lion that doesn't take himself too seriously.

This is how I see myself in my own movie, as an animal and as a person. In seeing myself as this spirit animal I can then also imagine myself today working on developing what I want to see more of in myself. That's the point after all, for this cheesy-wishy-washy-ness: to get results!

... and guess what we must do in order to get results. We must create something, not just anything, we must create a story: and it is not enough to just create a story in this scenario: we must craft the story to what we want to see more of!

How do you do this? I can't say for certain how each and every human should or would go about it, but I can tell you what may be of help to many.

Ask questions about yourself and answer them. Think about what you enjoy, what you're curious about, what you want to see more of... ask questions on how you can see more of it, proceed in this endless loop until you have crafted a story that gives you goosebumps or some sort of conviction. The goal is to compel yourself to do the things your movie character or spirit animal would do.

Start small: start with your first steps in the story i.e. where you were born, who your parents are, your first recollection of conscious thought... You know, the simple stuff... and then work up to where you are now, where you're going, where you want to go most, how you plan on getting there, how you have no idea on how you'll get there, what you'll do when times get tough, how you'll embody your spirit animals in the face of hardship, etc. etc.

At the end of the day a story is more so about how it makes you feel than what it is telling you logically. I didn't discover this until I was halfway done writing this book, so you may see the pace of some chapters change dramatically from logical steps to me grasping my own feelings and putting them onto the page.

In how this relates to you creating a convincing story or figuring out what your ideal spirit animal is... This means you should focus on what makes you feel compelled to take the first step, what parts of your story make you feel sad, mad, happy, frustrated: how did you overcome them, how will you overcome them. You don't have to write it all down (although it wouldn't hurt. Just think about the things that matter to you, and focus on them more in the light you want to see.

Creating or *crafting* a story that convinces you, by the feeling it brings, to live in your movie life, or your ideal animal spirit, this is where you may want to aim. Or not, you should do whatever feels convincing to you. **Where do you want to go? Who do you want to be? Only you can know, only you can see.**

- wow, I really got lucky with that last line, it rhymes, it flows. pretty proud of that creation, felt worthy of my craft (even though it was sort of an accident, a happy one!)

// afterword addition: this chapter is good to me and holds a lot of truth, but there is also an idea about us having different versions of ourselves that has caught my eye. So, perhaps one part of you that really wants a cheeseburger is a hippopotamus and the other part of you who wants to eat a healthy salad is a deer... this is to say that we may be composed of many different characters or animals. This train of thought is pretty cool to me as it's useful to take our lives a little less seriously, and reap more joy as opposed to grimness about which animal we are or who we are. This line of thinking may be just a fun thought to you, but you may also find it valuable, so here I've put it.

thirty-one.

Lacking inspiration?

When I told the world (my internet friends) that I was writing this book, one of them asked that I cover a particular question they had about creating things. The question was: *"What stuff to do when you don't have deep and constant inspirations of doing something?"*

There is no magic key to create things. Inspiration is by large perishable. If you don't act on inspiration promptly it will fade, and when it does fade (which it always does) you will have to continue on in the dark without your light to guide you.

If inspiration was our guideline or main source of light to get through doing things then we wouldn't have gotten anywhere near where we are today. The truth is that inspiration is not light at all, it's a spark at times that may help us see there is indeed a path surrounding us, but it is not a large enough light to keep us on the path.

The thing that guides us in the dark is a *why*. The thing that compels us to traverse the dark is a good reason. The guide is the reason, or rather: the purpose for doing something. After all is said and done you will only feel like doing something worthwhile some of the time, the other times you must grit through. The easiest way to grit through is to have a why, or a reason. There is little sense in subjecting yourself to displeasure without an intention or reason behind such subjection.

In the middle of the night you don't want to leave your cozy warm bed, but you have a really good reason too... you have to pee! The why is stronger than the comfortable state you're in, so you break out of your comfort to ease the discomfort of having to pee.

This analogy isn't perfect, but neither will be the circumstances when you have to do something you don't want to do. There is no perfect timing coming, and waiting for inspiration is a sunk cost most of us could wait our whole lives waiting for. The truth is I don't think inspiration comes to us, most of the time I think we create it.

So to answer the question: *"What stuff to do when you don't have deep and constant inspirations of doing something?"*:

If you lack inspiration you must do some things and make some noise in hopes of creating some inspiration. When you just do something, you make some noise, you tend to end up on one of two paths. The first path being that you just did some stuff and you don't feel particularly inspired about it all, but you did some stuff and it's something you wouldn't have done if you had been paralyzed about your own lack of inspiration. The second path is that you did some stuff, you made some noise, and you caught a bit of inspiration along the way too (lucky you!) This inspiration caused you to do some more stuff. On both paths where you started with no inspiration, you still managed to [do some stuff]. And that's really all we can aim for, in my friendly opinion. To do some stuff means that you're making waves, you're making noise, and in this way people can find you, or you can find more of yourself, and in turn you will be able to find more inspiration and make more progress.

If I'm lucky, one day every week I'll wake up and feel inspired to create some things, to do some stuff. On all the other days of the week I have to just do some stuff and go from there. I have to ***just get started*** (feel free to go back and read that chapter now too).

To put my views on inspiration simply: we cannot wait for inspiration, life will end up passing us by all too quickly, we must instead go and make some noise, we must do some stuff, and create inspiration for ourselves.

We must put fuel in our tank so we can continue doing stuff so that we can put more fuel in our tank.

A final note for this reality is also this: *You may not always feel like doing stuff, this doesn't necessarily mean that you need to push yourself to do something. Maybe you genuinely don't need to do some things. So take note of what you're doing and why you're doing it, then you can evaluate whether the stuff you are resisting doing was worthwhile in the first place. To best evaluate these things you will need to first know what you want, and then zoom out. All of this final note is easier said than done, so I'm just going to leave it here as a gentle reminder.*

thirty-two.

The right way, or the wrong way, or your way?

Any way will do, just pick a way and get going. Have you ever been at a crossroads between what you should be doing versus what you are doing? Have you ever wondered if the path you're taking is headed the right way? Have you ever wondered how anyone could know which way is truthfully the right way or the wrong way? (this is in terms of your life's pathway, not which side of the road you should be driving on, or which is the right way to go north)

Well, me too. And one persistent thing that I can't seem to shake from my own curiosity, and here I am putting into yours now... *how can anyone know what is the correct way about one's life more so than the person living it?*

Truthfully there are some obvious rebuttals to this question: but let's put aside logic for a moment, let's traverse this question with a sort of feeling instead...

Have you ever experienced your intuition working for you? Suddenly you have information about something you paid no attention to consciously but you still know something is off. You can feel that something is not quite right about the guy walking towards you, or you feel someone staring at you from behind and when you turn around, there they are, staring!

These are things we cannot explain, and I know you have experienced this same sense of intuition. For example: when someone tells us we should do things a certain way, but in our hearts we know there is another way, there is our way: which to many may look like the wrong way, or the only way, but in reality it is our way… and if it is wrong, then guess what: it's still our way, and now we can adjust our own way to go where we want to go, so long as we don't throw in the towel.

Or maybe it is time to throw in the towel, maybe your way was the way of realizing that something is not worth your time, that you would rather focus your attention on something else you're curious about. There is no sense in traversing through life with a constant agony about how you're committed to finishing something you started but now realize you don't enjoy whatsoever. There's no trophy and little glory if any at all in such an endeavor (caveat: you're in a marathon).

But the only way to get over this dilemma of finding your own way, finding what you really enjoy, is to get on about starting and figuring out what way you want to go as you go, as you make mistakes, as you conquer skills and as you fall flat on your face. You must get going in any way you can in order to keep going on your way.

Coming back to our question again (I know I went on a little of a rant there): *how can anyone know what is the correct way about one's life more so than the person living it?*

The truth is, they can't! Someone may have a good idea for a "right way" a person can take, but there is almost always another way of getting the same results by taking a different route. It may be perceived as harder, or easier to the person gate keeping someone from trying, but nonetheless it should be up to the person who owns their own life to make it how they want it (or how they think they want it).

Whether one way is more right than another doesn't matter all that much. In the end, all that matters is that someone is interested in the way they're going. If they aren't interested, or they aren't curious about what comes next, then they will not stay on their own way for long enough to get to where they want to go… and that would mean that the right way for one person prescribed to another person ended up failing the person trying to find their own "right way".

To explore your own way is a gift of life, it may not work out cleanly, it may be a mess of sorts, you may get some mud on yourself, but you owe it to you, to find your own way: because that's where all the treasure lies. (Or at least that's my way of thinking, maybe you think there is more to this all, maybe you don't want to follow my way, that's great too, do you boo.)

If you do end up finding the "right way" for going about life, feel free to share it loudly, but also know this: Telling someone how you found the right way is like sharing your winning lottery ticket, it's not transferable, the spoils are redeemed by the winner, and the only way to be a winner in this game is to find your own way. You can tell people how you went about acquiring your lottery ticket, maybe something sticks with them, but do they even want to win your lottery? Or is your win their eternal hell?: These are all things to consider.

It's worth noting that you can find your own way by seeing how others you admire have found their way, and reverse engineer from there. In this sense the winning lottery ticket is not entirely useless, but you have to look at the processes someone takes to get to where they are, and most of that is unknown, how can you know how a person thinks? What did they think about most to get to where they are? You just can't know these things. You can ask sure, but even the winners who have found a way don't entirely know how they got there. So you'll have to find what works best for you, you'll have to find your own way. You will have to try things and fall flat on your face; straight into the mud.

To me this is an exciting thing to think about. Putting yourself as the sculptor of your own path, however messy it may be, means you aren't nearly as helpless as you might have thought. It also means that you don't need to follow the same path that everyone else thinks you should, or even the paths of the people you aspire to be like.

Knowing you can take your own way and see how it works isn't saying that you'll get it "right" the first time around, heck you may never get it "right".

However, In taking your own approach you can proceed with your life knowing that you aren't just falling into a pit of what everyone else told you to do, you can instead bask in the light of your own new way of life, your own path. Some of it may ring true to what others know to be right, some of it may not, it doesn't matter really. What does matter is that your way of life can bring you a sense of peace, to know that you are following your own natural way, your curiosity, your sense of self. This to me is something that I still can't fully put into words, it's just a feeling of faith really, faith in yourself that your intuition or your curious brain has a way of figuring things out. The main goal for me is to just keep on my own way, playing this game of sorts, for as long as I can, forever.

The wrong way to create vs the right way vs your way

This book is mainly about creation, and creating things... So I would be remiss to not include in this chapter something about how this relates to the book's overarching message that you are built to create stuff.

When it comes to creating things, again, there is no wrong way to create. I may have my own set of biases on what I want to create, and how I want to create it, but that doesn't mean what you create has to follow my own notions of correctness.

In general: Creation is the process of adding something to the world that was not there before. Creation could be you phoning your mom, this creates a conversation, a connection, a bond, and memories.

Your form of creation can be extremely different from mine, and extremely different from Bob's (Bob is a random name I have picked here, if your name is Bob and you're reading this: hello Bob!)... it doesn't matter. What does matter? That you are creating things! And that you are on your own way about it! Your "own way" may be imitating or even copying something someone else made (there are a lot of lessons to be learned when trying to replicate someone's creations). What matters is that you've begun the act, you've picked a way and you're on it now.

Just like finding the "right" way of life, the right way to create things is less about what you're creating and more so about you creating something, anything at all.

thirty-three.

My vision of creation, for reference

A look into my head: It began a long time ago, in a not-so-distant land (earth), I was created by my mom. I plopped out and said, "I'm going to write a book, and make this really cool app, and write about awesome useful things, and explore my curiosities, oh yes all of these wonderful things I shall begin my quest, onwards, starting now!" ha-ha no, I'm *just kidding*, obviously, because I couldn't talk until my later years of being a big ol' baby.

Here we are today, I'm 23 years old, and only **now** can I tell you what I'm here to do, what this book and what my past work this year has been all about, what I've come to realize over the course of two rapid decades.

I want to change the world's view on "work", and above this I want to add more of three sparsely spread infections: Curiosity, Creativity, Joy, and Love... Okay I lied it's four, I think baby me came up with this plan, which must be why I miscounted.

First, as mentioned on changing the view of "work" I want to do a few things in this regard, and I hope my book has helped you see yourself some possibilities that you hadn't yet discovered yet on your own for what "work" entails. The gist is this: my goal is to help people find work that looks like play, and see that what is work can also be a play. Framing/perspective is everything. This feat is no small feat, to find something you would love to explore, to participate in, to have fun while doing so, and all while this fun is ongoing to have someone think what you're doing is just so dreadful, it's too much "work". My first step in helping people find some form of work that feels like play has been my writing, and a large part of this is building a super cool app (which may ultimately fail, as all things may), but first: my writing. What am I doing to help encourage this type of work that feels like play? Well, I'm cheering for curiosity.

Curiosity is a gateway drug to exploring work that feels like play, or possibly better put, curiosity is the breadcrumbs of your life's work, your great work: both of which often come from work that feels like play. And oh man what joy it brings one's soul to do great work, to have one's brain cells infused with one's hands in perfect unison, to be completely involved in a craft or working endeavor. It feels good, and it feels **great** when this line is gotten to in a curious manner.

Many people seem to think curiosity killed the cat, but little people know that satisfaction brought it back! Seriously, I didn't know of this other half of the saying until I was 22 years old and had already been reprimanded for asking too many questions on multiple occasions. I wish I had known this other half when I was younger. Because the ability to ask questions, especially when it makes you look silly, is a child's super strength. The one who asks questions curiously is fond on finding out the answers, they are fond on learning, and most people think learning is just "too much work". So already you can see the upwards hill you are traveling on by simply asking questions (ask them to yourself too, curiosity is your best friend.) I would always encourage someone to be curious, it's a very worthwhile thing to be.

Now, on the "me creating a super cool app" side of things, here's my honest master plan with creating such a thing. First off, I am not a super experienced programmer, I have some basic knowledge, but for 99% of the things I need to do I'm going to have to learn how to do them as a complete beginner. Note: To make an application of sorts like the one I want to make I will need to know how to program it myself or pay someone a lot of money to do it for me. Today as I write this marks the second week of me learning how to program and yesterday, I launched my applications information page with a waitlist. If the app is still living, you can find it at curiosityquench.com → **go see for yourself what has come of my creation. The thing is, although this app to me is what I've always wanted: a way to find new interests and get actionable tips on how to try said interests, I'm not sure how it will play out for other people. Here's the thing though, why I'm creating it without any certainty that it will bring me a bunch of money, or anything at all, I'm creating it because to me it feels like I just *must*** find out. I must find out if this is something I can build, I must learn some more skills so I can create more wild things I have locked up in my head. I have to build this thing to learn those skills, and I have to create something I am curious about because I believe that is exactly what my mission is here on this earth; well that, and spreading lots of love, joy, creativity, and curiosity to others, of course (can't keep it all to myself, that would be no fun).

As you can see by my long wall of text, I am trying to enable people to be more curious. That's the general gist of my master plan on top of my loving and joyful motives. The reason I want people to be curious segways nicely into love and joy, but it also is a prerequisite for one to enjoy their human abilities. Specifically, their human ability to create things. After all, **you were built to create.**

In all, and I'll tell you now: The master plan is for myself to create a book, a blog, video log, and an app that helps Inspire more people to create more things, through first helping them discover what they are curious about and then setting them free from there with a wave of encouragement to do what compels them.

Setting them free because anyone who has discovered or rediscovered their sense of curiosity and genuinely follows it, they will end up creating all sorts of things as a byproduct of their exploration. That's where I am today, I asked a question to myself, I asked it to the world (the world did not give me an answer, nor did I have the answer, I still don't) and now I am on my way to not just find answers, but to find new questions to ask. I ended up creating this book, I ended up on a path of learning, and I somehow stumbled upon doing a bunch of work that feels like play to me. The wonders of it all really. It all came from a simple seed of curiosity.

My overarching philosophy, also known as the "frik it filosophy" is below for you to read:

→ Follow your genuine curiosity
→ Create often
→ Live a better life (one with more joy and love, of course)
Honorary mentions: Love thyself, Encourage others.

Sidenote: This philosophy is still developing to me, so some words may change around still, I'm not completely sure: how can anyone ever be completely sure? Maybe it won't change, I don't know, how could I know? I just create things and let them be, until I want to change them: there is not enough capacity in me to worry about it all that much, that I may want to change something later but I can't.

How my creations are proponents of this mission: I was going to write this section, but I think all of the above outlines exactly how what I'm creating here is a proponent of my mission, today is the 21st of September, the year is 2023, and as these are my 1500 words I have created today, I rest this creation here, *for you,* your honor.

And finally for this chapter, here is a parting mini pep talk affirmation woo-woo bit, just for you:

You were built to create cool shit, so please, go do that! The world would love to see your soul on your sleeve, trust me. Your own self would love to see more of yourself too. Those who laugh at you or make fun are wearing a fake soul on their sleeve as their real one is being used to patch over their heart of broken dreams.

So go dream, create things, be curious as to what the world has for you (a lot more than you think). On the way you may also open the eyes to others' broken dreams that all hope is not yet lost... "there is still light for we are still creating things".

thirty-four.

The Do 100 approach

Figuring out what you enjoy and how you can get better. A great approach to building your own body of experience/skills (your life portfolio) is to do 100 of a thing, multiple things. This methodology was first brought to me by a guy on twitter, and as that is, I'm going to use his guidance for this chapter. You can read Visakan Veerasamy's original blog post [here](#) titled "do 100 things". Nonetheless, I'm going to go over it here, how it's helped me, and how I believe it can help you on your journey.

First, here are some examples of this approach in practice to give you a good outlook on the general idea of such a simple approach of "do it 100 times." …

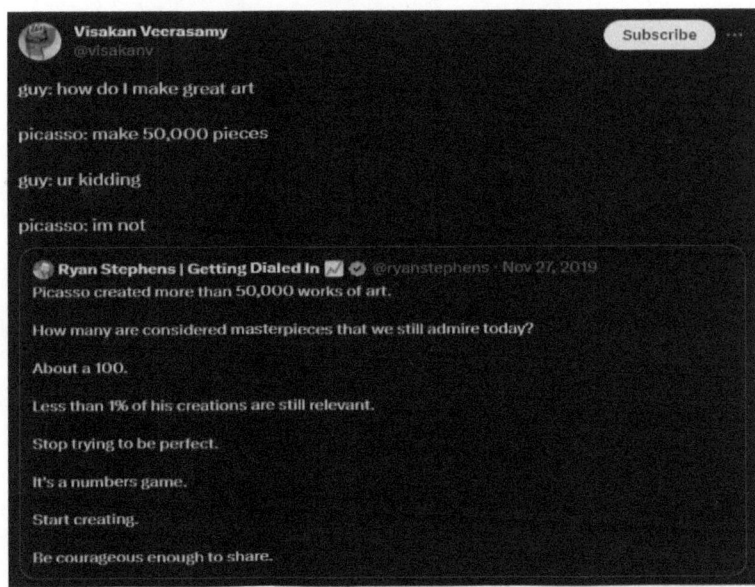

Picasso's advice to you, if you want to get better at art, is really just: create more art. Seems simple enough right? Where else does this apply?

Running:

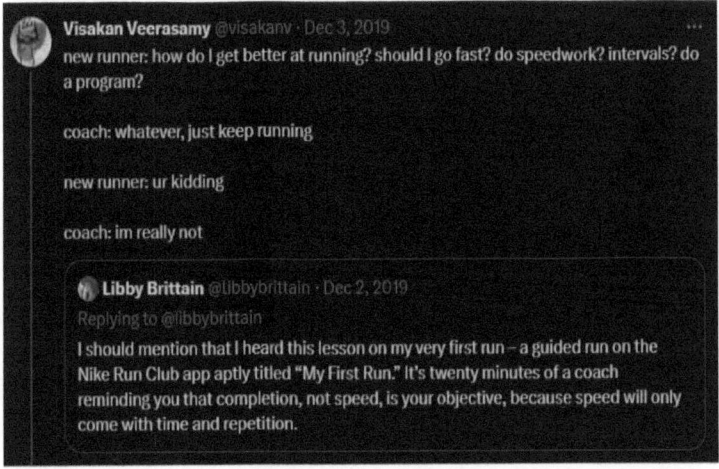

Making videos on the internet (vlogging):

Visakan Veerasamy @visakanv · Dec 7, 2019
vlogger: how to become youtube famous

some swedish guy: make 3,000 videos

> **Visakan Veerasamy** @visakanv · Apr 4, 2019
> Replying to @visakanv
> I sometimes joke "who is this Pewdiepie person, never heard of him" – but the fact is he has published over THREE THOUSAND AND SEVEN HUNDRED VIDEOS. IMO, make and publish 1,000+ of "anything" before you gripe about missing some boat or hype train. Makers are usually busy making.

Writing:

Visakan Veerasamy @visakanv · Dec 7, 2019
how become really good writer who comes outta nowhere

> **Visakan Veerasamy** @visakanv · Mar 27, 2019
> TIL that @morganhousel wrote 3,382 articles for fool dot com before I had ever heard of him and thought "wow who's this really good writer who came outta nowhere"
>
> fool.com/investing/2016...

Podcasting:

Visakan Veerasamy @visakanv · Dec 29, 2019
Do 1,400 podcast episodes

> **George Mack** ✓ @george__mack · Dec 27, 2019
> If you're afraid of putting ideas out there, watch this - @joerogan's FIRST EVER podcast
>
> The first 10 minutes is him struggling to connect to the internet
>
> It's horrific
>
> 10 years of compounding growth later and he gets 100+ million downloads per month
>
> youtube.com/watch?v=ZWBCnv...

Building a pitch deck for investors:

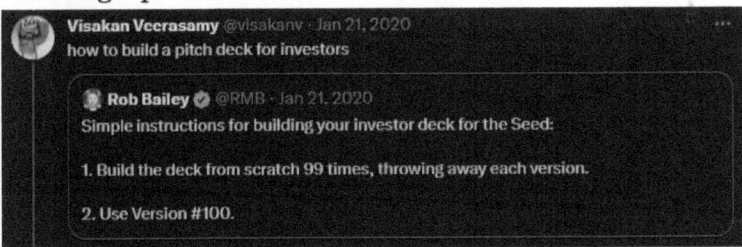

Selling chocolate bars (doing business)

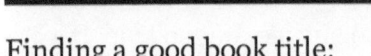

Finding a good book title:

Becoming a musician:

And there are infinitely more examples of this approach, but I think you get the gist of it now. Or I hope so... In case you don't "get it" all quite yet, here is how our friendly internet friend Visakan put's it so it can't be misconstrued:

"Do 100 Crappy Things For No Reason, With No Agenda To Live Up To, At Whatever Pace Feels Comfortable, However You Like." – *Visakan Veerasamy*

// reminder: you can also just not do a thing, you don't have to do anything you don't want to.

Honestly I don't really think there is much more I can add to this chapter. The concept is so simple, but so true. It's almost like everything is connected to, like Nike says, just doing it (the thing, whatever the thing may be).

But please, keep in mind this: you don't need to do 100 of anything just because you started 10 of a thing. You may find out after doing 5, or 3 or 19 of a thing that you'd rather spend your time doing 100 of something else. By all means, go be curious in another domain. The point of doing 100 to me is largely a vehicle for realizing what you might want to do 100 of, and a vehicle for curiosity about "what would it look like to do 100 of this thing?" maybe you'll be better off, maybe not... how can you know? Well you can try to do 100 things 100 times, it would be unlikely that you come out of this experience without a ton of, well... *experience.*

"When you switch on the dirty tap, shit water is going to flow out for a substantial amount of time. Then clean water will start to flow out." — **Ed Sheeran**

With Ed's quote in mind: If you were to do 100 of something, any-thing, don't you think your dirty tap would spout a little more clean water than it did before you did 100 of that thing? At some point, some bits of clean water are bound to make their way through, you just need to keep the tap on long enough to get it all out. Do 100 of a thing, see what happens, do ten of a thing, or five, do the thing, see what happens. Who knows what will happen? Only the doer of things knows.

To wrap this up let's think about creating 100 things. As of now you may be creating things from time to time, but what if you declared "I am going to make 100 things!" well now you are on your way, and the first step, the only step to make yourself more on your way is to do the thing, to create something.

For me I did this with YouTube videos, I created one every day, (you don't need to do daily, this was just the approach I chose) and in a matter of six months I was in a place of progress I had no idea could have come from this approach of just doing 100. My expectations at first were set high, but as I put the expectations aside, the experience became much more fun. I was having fun just doing the thing every day, whatever may come of it. It was a reward in itself to do the thing, and that's how I ended up making 1200 YouTube videos in three years.

Oddly enough If I look back into my life and the things I've created that have been to my notation of "worthwhile" all of these things stem from some variation of "do the thing, a lot of times". I figured out the things I didn't want to do in this way, I continued on doing the things I did want to do this way, and I even optimized my health in this way. I did these things, lots of times.

A final example for this chapter which put me in a sort of awe is this example of Visakan Veerasamy drawing an owl and his progression in "doing the thing". See how doing the things leads to his faucet getting clear water (there was dirty water to get out of his system).

Visakan's first three owl drawings:

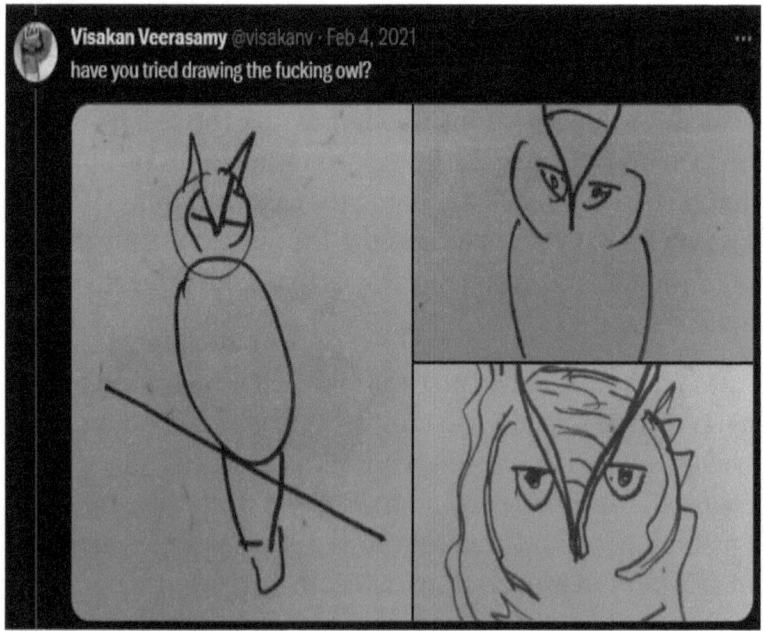

Visakan's 9th owl drawing:

As you can see, it didn't take all that long to get significantly better at something. The biggest blockade is usually just your expectation that you can't do the thing enough times before you see progress. And maybe it takes longer to see progress than 9 doings of a thing, maybe it takes 100, but it's clear that progress is happening because how else would you get to your final form, if not to do a thing more? Each rep is a step forward... Not always up, but forwards.

Note: Visakan stopped at Owl 9, because he realized he didn't want to draw owls anymore.

thirty-five.

Growing up... it's not worth it?

"You don't actually need to "Know" what you want, in order to do what you want. Children certainly don't! They just do what they want! The problem is that we get inside our own heads. We force ourselves to justify ourselves." – Visakan Veerasamy

As I mentioned in the introduction of this book: *"our senses of wonder, curiosity, imagination... are all often flushed away by the idea that we should 'grow up'."*

Now, I want to revisit this important dilemma, to grow up, or not to grow up... it's such a popular tassel we humans seem to face as we settle into our monotonous and cushy lives. Many people will pose that you should grow up when you're acting silly, or rambunctious. Being a child-like adult mostly means that you are embracing that you just can't help from enjoying all the wonders of the world, throwing the idea of saving a serious face to the wind, who cares if you are to be wondrous as a child is at times, how is this such a terrible act? It isn't, but many will try to trip you up, many may try to knock you into their frame of renounced wonder... let me tell you now, it's not worth it, to grow up.

Naturally, we all grow up, you can't help it! But in the sense of being told to grow up when you're only trying to have a little fun: a water balloon fight, chasing water slides, or doing other non-water fun activities. Who wants to renounce these sorts of things? Why should we not have a little fun? Why can't we embrace the curious wonder inside of us? We can! And we can do it as adults as we did children.

There are many good rebuttals to these questions, and the most common one seems to be "You're too old for that", too old to have some fun? Well, I'll be curiously turning my coffin to that reasoning! Haha, oh so funny how we humans want to renounce for others what we think we cannot have for ourselves. It's silly really. And I've done it too! I wanted to eat less junk food and sugars, so I tried to impose my will on others: but this is not how the world works. Not as far as I can tell so far, if you think strongly otherwise: I would love to chat about it.

In totality my conclusion has been this: It is not worth the cost to "grow up", it is much better to keep your inner child with you, even if it makes people look at you funny from time to time. Their will of the way forwards is theirs, not yours.

Please note that when I say "It is not worth growing up", what I really mean is that we would often benefit from retaining many of our child-like qualities as we grow older. They are vital to bringing us and the rest of the world more joy. Your creative, and curious spirit is worth keeping alive much more so than how all together you appear to others; that's the gist of my point, not that you shouldn't take on more responsibility as you grow older or do grown up things. Growing old is inevitable, losing your sense of wonder is not.

Changing perspective from growing up vs not growing up, someone left me this reply which I thought was a fresh way of seeing the whole ordeal:

(good extra layer with the pun there too)

To be honest even the people who say they have renounced their child like wonder, the ones who claim to be all grown up and far past being able to take part in all sorts of fun activities (water sports included), these people are liars. They are trying to save face because someone else convinced them they should be a big fancy grown up. Their tree trunk still contains the layer of their inner child, they may have wrapped many years of layers on top of it, but it's still there. In this sense they still have it with them, they may have to dig a little deeper to undo their stuck-up grown-up pants, but it can be done no doubt: for the layer is still there with them, and it never left. Friendly and genuine encouragement goes a long way here: to help others enjoy themselves in ways they may be hiding from.

No matter who you are, this means you also can explore your curiosity to its childlike end, you can ask questions that others find silly, you can be a dazzling fool (the intentional fool quickly becomes wise from his mistakes and lessons).

This also means no one is stopping you from creating things that you may have wanted to create but hesitated to, because you didn't want to seem childish. You like Lego and want to build some sick ass Lego sets? Why the hell not? Why shouldn't you? Maybe there is some real logic there, but most blockades to doing things that are actually fun but slightly childish go something like "I'm a big fancy grown up with grown up pants, I couldn't possibly use these big fancy grown up pants to play with Legos" – Get over yourself you big baby!

My grown-up idol as a kid was exactly who it is today, it's the grown up who is going with the wills of their own way, the one who was a lot more likely to encourage me and join me in my activities as opposed to being the grown up who has their pants done up too high and mighty to do something *just for fun*. You don't need unlimited bandwidth for fun, but it's enjoyable to have more than most adults.

> // An afterword addition to this chapter: I also want to mention how a lot of growing up **is actually worth it**. For example: the fulfillment for long term things is gained through not just following your instincts or what feels good in the moment, but rather these things are pursued and gained in succession through a higher level of consciousness. Not a lower one.
>
> Many child-like qualities would consist of a sense of ignorant bliss, the adult version of embracing child-like fun is not so much the same in this sense. The child-like part of being an adult is also still valuable to itself. But being able to have fun comes largely when you're an adult because you are more aware, not less, of your own peril if you aren't to have fun... which is the opposite of being a child. So to avoid growing up into a grumpy non fun

*adult, the goal is really just to be more conscious. This is something I'm still figuring out. If you're interested in this line of thinking, then checkout these books below too (and then take action on the advice: this is something that must be learned through trial and error. And as far as I know it will take years and years of consistent effort.) Book recommendations: "**The Power of Now**" by Eckhart Tolle, and "**Flow**: The Psychology of Optimal Experience" by Mihaly Csikszentmihalyi.*

Perhaps this chapter was framed in an odd way for these conclusions, I'm not sure yet, but I hope you can see my brain matter exposed here.

thirty-six.

Have you tried just having fun?

Speaking of doing things *just for fun*...

"Just have fun" - is something Richard Williams said often to his girls when raising them to be the top tennis players in all of the sport's history. And you've likely heard the names, Venus Williams and Serena Williams if you've ever turned on any sports channel ever. Even if not, you still may be reading this thinking *"Just have fun, really? That's the motto preached to raise two of the world's best tennis players?"*

Well, yep. Just have fun is the motto and in this chapter I want to go deeper into this motto to outline:

- Why having fun matters a lot.
- How to have more fun.
- The real winner's mentality behind fun.

All so you can make your own conclusions and philosophy around trying to add more fun into your life.

Why fun matters

Most of the people living life as adults have lost the light for fun, their sense of child-like fun is all but dimmed down to nothing. This is an absolute shame because fun matters, and it matters a lot. Imagine yourself living a life without fun, everything is all work, no play. Imagine you can go to an all-inclusive resort somewhere tropical, but you can't leave your room and you must work 8 hours each day. This to me is how most adults are choosing to lead their lives. All around them are all these fun things, hobbies, activities, and possible pursuits of wonder, and yet they stay mentally in a mode where they are locked in the same, all-work no-play room all day long.

Of course, nothing ought to be fun all the time, you will have your off days where you feel like doing nothing or you face some struggle: But FUN as a focus for doing things is an excellent one.

Sadly a lot of adults will scorn people for having fun, for getting lost in an activity like a child, this is because they have pushed their own fun so far back into the dark pit of their soul that it has grown into hatred for itself (dark, I know).

Going back to the biography of Richard Williams "King Richard" for a second: There are many points of the film that berates the average tennis parent. The parents who scream and get angry at their kid when their kid loses, as opposed to Richard's approach which was to make sure his kid's "just had fun".

Funnily enough the fun aspects and focus on the fun are what also made the not-so-fun aspects of the two tennis stars' journeys fun, they fell in love with all the fun parts of tennis, and the things that looked like immense work to others ended up feeling like play to them.

Having fun matters ultimately, not because it makes you a better person, or helps you enjoy every waking hour of your life, but rather it matters because it stops you from questioning yourself and lets you enjoy the moment you are in fully a lot more often.

This is one of my ideas on why fun matters, but feel free to draw your own conclusions about why else fun matters too. If you focus on fun, you will find more of it; like anything you put your focus on. So figure out your focus, and make it fun.

Finding fun in the boring stuff

Just the other day, I was at the beach with my girlfriend and best friend. We were all sitting on a towel, trying to warm up after swimming in the cold water near the backside of the beach.

While we were warming up we had a show put on for us where we watched two kids no older than ten having an overbearing amount of fun doing something most would consider absolutely boring. and they only stopped when their mom called them back, they were in an adrenaline rush trance level of fun, I could tell because I remember the feeling from when I was a kid. What were they doing?

They were throwing rocks, aiming to hit a foam football moving with the coming and going tide on the shore. That's all, they didn't have any fancy slingshots or gadgets. They picked up a rock, took aim at the foam football, then jumped (and screamed) in excitement every time they got close to hitting the ball.

Why was it equally fun just to watch them have fun?

— *Think about it for yourself before reading on for 10 seconds* —

It was equally fun because they weren't doing anything I couldn't do, yet they made it into an absolute adventure, a sport, and a fantastical event with every second: one couldn't help to have fun just watching others having fun at such heights.

How to have more fun

This section doesn't need to be long because I've already covered how to have more fun.

Here's the "answer":

Focus your life around fun, Focus on having fun, and you will naturally have more of it; Like anything you put your focus on.

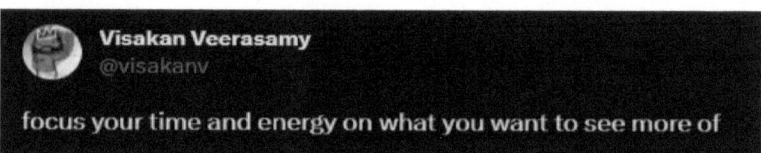

The winner's mentality behind having fun

Having fun is also a winners mentality, and luckily it's not very complicated. Here's what I mean: People who are having fun naturally don't feel like they are partaking in a chore or work even when to others it may appear like what they are doing for fun is a lot of work or effort.

a focus of having fun ultimately leads to the achievement and finding the answers of these quotes listed below from Naval

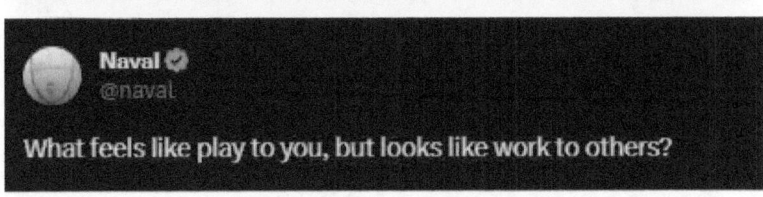

The winner's mentality behind having fun is that you find something that feels like play to you, but looks like work to others.

The example we've been using so far carries over: Someone who is playing tennis for fun, or treating it foremost as their form of play will have a much higher likelihood or honing in on the craft than someone who is just doing it as a form of work.

The person who is playing tennis and feels like it is work will not outcompete someone who is in a state of play. One person is depleted by the "work" of tennis while the other person is energized by the "work" because it is their form of fun and play. That's the winner's mentality of fun. The fun-haver trumps the worker for concerted effort into just about anything.

If you really want to boil this chapter down, the lesson is simple… "***Just have fun***".

thirty-seven.

Effortless creation? Lightweight Curiosity?

This chapter is kind of a rant, maybe it will help you.

Creating things is awesome, I think I've mentioned that somewhere in this book already, right? I know this book is kind of a mess in a sense of congruency but let me give you some insight as to why... so you may see a different way of creation than the way you have predefined in your head.

First off, this book is sort of a mess because my creation genes are very moment to moment focused. I often get so lost in creating things or writing the words in this book that I completely forget that my entire purpose of this book is to inspire anyone who reads it to pick themselves up and create something. In all honesty I don't necessarily want someone to keep reading as much as I'd prefer to transpire creation in someone.

With that in mind I have come to write this rant of a chapter. It may not make complete sense, but this is *my* form of effortless creation. An effortless creation is not creation with no effort whatsoever, rather it's getting into a groove, with substantial effort, and then being able to flow with the groove to stay in it. This process could be described in similarity to the effort it takes to climb a large hill in the snowy winter, and then the following ease it takes to slide back down it.

As you read this, I have taken the steps up the snowy hill to frame in my mind this chapter, and now as I write I am sliding down the hill at a rapid pace, picking up speed, and retaining momentum until I ultimately reach the bottom of the hill. Why am I telling you this? I'm not sure. I think it's mostly because the most effective advice is not advice at all, rather it's a description of inner workings, or a lived experience, a display: of someone's self in the process of embodying the advice they wish to preach.

I'm urging anyone who picked up this book to create some stuff, and in order to ask something of you, would it not make sense to show you how I go about it all? To show you my path so you can take step one of it and then decide the next for yourself? I think this makes more sense than me telling you to just go and create some stuff, hoping you feel what I have felt in creating things for no reason at all. Instead of me hoping you find the same lessons, this chapter is me only hoping you see my lessons and feel curious enough to make your own conclusions by creating something yourself.

If I have gotten off track about creation I apologize, but many of the chapters that are not directly related to creation and why *you're built to create* are more so a display of my own creations. They are here to show you what I write is a creation of my own will, not that it fits in this book perfectly, but that it's the only way I could have written this book while in the exploration of my own curiosity. Perhaps this book is selfish in that regard.

Something is effortless about creation specifically when it aligns with curiosity. Sure, I may have told myself to write

1000 words on this very book each day, but I did this with curiosity. Anything I was curious about that I had on my mind I put it in this book during the days of its writing. This is what made this book's creation have many effortless moments. There is a lack of resistance when you are in line with your curiosity, to me it's like an innate sense of "I want to learn, I want to try, it does not matter what does or doesn't come from my efforts. I just wish to explore".

This is a powerful experience to have, and changes you compared to just thinking about it. Mainly because the person actually experiencing this feeling of curiosity, is the person who takes on the quest to quench it. This person must be in the act of being in the present, they have no time to worry, no time to feel sorrow, no time to exclaim about what may come of tomorrow. It may be only for a brief moment, but there is a time when the curious explorer cannot think of anything but the quest they are on, the quest to quench their curiosity. This feeling is joyous and fun, it's a feather in the wind compared to the anchor of disinterest you may otherwise have about the world around you.

In this weird effortless sense when you are curious, you are free. The weight of your spirit is lighter, yet it's harder to move you in a bothersome way. Your curiosity is not just adverse to resistance, it's completely indifferent about it.

The great part about all of this is you can be curious all you want, it's a wonderful approach to be a part of. To wonder in a positive way.

That's all for this rant, I was curious as to where it would lead. Now this is the end, the end of my effortless descent down a snowy winter hill. To the next chapter.

thirty-eight.

The purpose of beauty and it's creations

// I have removed 1500+ words from this chapter, here lay the cookie crumbs that Santa left behind.

Your creations will need you to help them find their beauty, they need you to create them so they may blossom.

The mushy bits of life are your friends: for beauty can transpire positive change when nothing else can.

Pictured below is a lotus flower, growing through the mud, the swamp, and the harshest conditions. Despite all of the weight against the flower, it blossoms. Very similar to you and your creations.

thirty-nine.

Giving light to the grim reaper

The grim reaper is you, show it light, let it prosper into a reaper of joy. There are a lot of times when I look too far ahead of myself and end up tripping or stubbing my toe.

This happens in both the physical sense and the mental sense. In this chapter we'll be talking in the mental sense. The mental version of stubbing a toe is much more grim, as mental darkness can spiral much more rapidly. It can become a monster of our reality, quickly eating up all of our hope.

To avoid the spiral of our own darkness, to turn our own grim reaping into joyous reaping, we need to give our darkness light. How do we give it light? How do we turn the grim reaper inside of us into a joyous reaper? Let us explore these questions, and possibly find some answers too…

You've probably had a moment or two in your life when everything just seemed so tiresome. A "what's the point" attitude or a "it's all doomed" outlook. This is you as the grim reaper talking, this is you saying to yourself that the future does not look convincing enough, that it does not look like things will work out. You are not compelled, clearly. This is common, or at least it has been to me in some points of my life. I've found myself consulting with the grim more than I like to admit.

But let's not forget about the other side of grim: joy. To find joy you cannot look ahead too far, at least not when you're *just getting started*. Instead you have to look at where you are now. Not *just* where you are now, but **only** where you are now. Looking at the here and now, without looking at where you *want* to go in X time.

If you look too far ahead you'll quickly fall back to the grim side of your fate, you'll not be able to think of the how, so you'll assume it just can't be done.. You'll think things cannot get better because you can't see how they will. This is the grim reaper trap, but if you shine some light on this trap you can notice it's not up to you right now to figure out the how, rather it's up to you right now to figure out the first step you need to take.

This idea is put together quite well by Steve Jobs in this popular quote: *"You can't connect the dots looking forward; you can only connect them looking backwards. So you have to trust that the dots will somehow connect in your future. You have to trust in something - your gut, destiny, life, karma, whatever. This approach has never let me down, and it has made all the difference in my life."*

You have to trust something. In order to overpower the grim reaper you need to find a way to cultivate a sense of trust in yourself. A trust that the dots will connect at some point, later down the road, even if they don't appear to connect right now. Even if you can't figure out the "how" right now, you have to trust you will figure it out eventually. This way you can manage to take the first step on a long journey of steps, to a much less grim future. Where there is hope, where there is light, and where both can be used to scare away the grim reaper of darkness.

The more trust you cultivate in yourself, over time (don't ask how, just take the first step), the more your joyous reaper will inhabit the space where the grim reaper used to live. The more you believe in you, the more you can actually do.

Finally I'd like to add that I'm not someone who has yet to fully conquer my grim reaper, but this is what has helped me so far on my journey of making a bunch of dots… As of right now they don't all connect, but I'm sure one day, someday, eventually, they will… and my life has been a lot better since I adopted this outlook, as opposed to constantly feeding my internal reaper reasons to transpire more darkness than light (more grim rather than joy).

Create your own dots, and *cultivate what you want to see more of.* This is how you can make a more compelling day-to-day life, for the rest of your life.

forty.

Creating stuff to find thyself

If you end up creating a lot of things, then it is only natural you will find out a lot about yourself. The more you find out about yourself, or rather the deeper you are involved with your own spirit, the more in tune you will be with a sense of love for life, a love for tomorrow. This isn't always the case every day, or in every person. However there is a sense of progress granted to those doing things to dive further into themselves, and that's what a large part of creating things is to me.

Let's take an example such as losing weight. Everyone wants to lose weight, or be healthier, but how many people will get started? Never mind how many people will keep going, but how many people will just get started? Sure, you may set a new years resolution and create a plan, then you fall off: but you started! Most people don't even get that far. They may do nothing at all, and they will not find themselves in this state, they just won't. (unless it's in introspective thought, which is in turn doing something, *but this only works if it leads to action*) The best hope for someone who hasn't even tried is for them to try. Where on the other hand someone who tried and failed has infinitely more data to work with and introspect about, they have a notch on the scale, a pebble in the pond, equity in their own mind. They have created something here in making an attempt, they have created for themselves: experience!

And what better way to find yourself than through experience? That's really what a large part of any creation process is. It's someone doing something and that gives them that experience. You can create experiences that are probably not as valuable as another or enjoyable, but each time you do something or put in effort on something, you are in the process of making a worthy benchmark of yourself for your mind to be able to extrapolate from. This is incredibly useful especially if you take time to think about the hard questions life brings like: What do you want out of life? What don't you want out of life? Who do you want to be? Why do you want these things? – These types of questions are a lot easier to answer if you have created things, done things, and added more experience to yourself. This is not to say you need to try everything, it's only to say that effort is valuable, and shouldn't be completely disregarded when progress is non-existent or recursive.

The above spiral of thoughts I just laid out comes from a previous thought that is as follows. Everyone wants to lose weight, no one wants to do the work. Something similar to this is: everyone wants to find work that feels like play to them, but no one wants to do the work.

Finding work that feels like play takes considerable concentrated effort over a long period of [persistent] time, maybe even a lifetime. Or rather: finding the games in life you want to play forever, and finding a way to play them forever... These are modern battles of the typical human. These battles take a lot of attention, a lot of hard introspection, lengthy concentration on your own thoughts (or a concentration to get rid of your thoughts all together.)

Most of us can't stand to be in our own heads. Like when someone reminds you that you have to breathe and makes you self conscious about breathing (sorry), the same is held for when someone reminds you that you have thoughts running through your head and you can't stop them (most of us can't at least), you cannot help but feel agitated, you open up your phone and start scrolling to avoid the prison you've created inside. You do not want to face your demons, even if they were created by your own mind, your beautiful mind with so much wonder yet to be explored.

It's no wonder why easy quick hits of endless short video clips or social media likes overtake a fellow human's curiosity and drive, it feels like things are being learned, the search is going on for what ones heart desires, it doesn't require you to face any of the ugly thoughts you have in your head, but the delusion is only apparent when you step away to see all of the progress you feel is on the cusp is really you being stuck on a hamster wheel. Real progress is high energy, real progress is hard, but progress is also one of the greatest treasures this world has to offer us, so it would seem important to make some of it, would it not?

I *want* to fix this progress void, I'm **trying** to fix it for others. Will I be able to? I have no idea. I haven't tried enough nor have I thought about it for long enough. Interestingly enough, in my attempts so far trying to make something that can break such a vicious cycle, I have learned a lot about myself. I have learned things I might never have known about my motivations, my inner thirsts, things that were locked behind the walls of the monster I now seek to defeat.

And the only reason I've been able to learn more about myself? Well it's because I started doing stuff. Trying things and learning things relevant to this mission, and I've come to see many parts of how the world may work in new ways. Somehow I've ended up being more receptive to understanding how our brains work, why we do the things we do, and how one locks themselves up, how I lock myself up as a prisoner while simultaneously being the jailor. This all comes from me creating things, doing things. I have learned so much, made a tiny bit of progress, and am excited to continue my quest.

This is something I try not to take for granted, that I have the ability to go through this process of creation, of doing stuff. You have it too, you can reach progress, no matter how little, it will feel good. Progress though, unlike cheaply earned dopamine, is lasting, it's a reputation builder with yourself, and it implies that you did some stuff. Progress implies that you created something outside of yourself using your self, and that's exactly the point of what us humans were built to do is it not? To make progress, to create something that was not yet existing until we came along.

As you go through this you will find your own meanings for work, for making progress, you will find yourself in the rubble of failure and the valor of victory, and that too, is what it's all about: the process, the process which is a parent to the progress.

// This chapter is a little mushy, and it's a little all over the place. I've contemplated cutting it out but I'm going to leave it here and hope it shines some light into a single person's soul. After all, this is part of my process, to tell you how I wanted to get rid of this and then you can tell me how silly I am, or how I should have, or reflect on yourself that maybe you should just go do some stuff and

stop caring what other people think. That's all, on to the next chapter my friend!

forty-one.

Creating for money

This chapter is a different one, it's a tough one. Mainly because it strikes a little closer to my heart than I would like to admit, but also because the topic of having a job, working for yourself, being your own boss vs being someone else's employee... These things all have polarizing opinions surrounding them.

It would be silly of me to write a book about creation without talking a little bit about money right? Read this chapter as if I am your friend spilling my soul out, because to me, that's exactly what's going on here.
// If you have any questions or want to talk about life with me: you can message me directly on social media or via email, there's a very good chance I will respond.

As I write this book I live in my mom's basement. I worked at McDonalds for three years while I was in college, and dropped out of college in my third and final year. I was at the top of my class, but at the bottom of filling my soul's intuitive needs.

It's been almost three years since I dropped out of college. And while I still did get a diploma for two years of computer programming, I still have yet to pursue a job in that field... in any field. Why? The punchline goes something like "I want to create something for myself, work for myself, make my own hours, and express my soul and creativity in my work, and I want to enjoy working for the rest of my life by doing work that feels like play to me".

Yeah... it's a lot. Many people reading this are probably thinking of throwing this book aside knowing this, so maybe I'm risking losing you as a reader, someone I value dearly. But I need to be truthful here when it comes to using your means of creation as a force for work, or a job...

It is not easy... it's **hard.**

But guess what? As you already may know... none of life after school is particularly *easy.* Just like you've heard shouted a million times by now in cheesy catchphrases and motivational speeches, you have to *"choose your hard!"*.

This chapter is for anyone who is thinking about using their creative abilities in relation to making money or providing value to others. If you don't care to search deeply for work that feels like play, or you already enjoy what you do to deliver value and earn money, then feel free to skip this chapter. I know for certain that these ideals are not matched for everyone, and each person has their own perfect day.

My perfect day includes work regardless of how wealthy I am, because to me the craft and the process is my work and that is also my play. If I can figure out ways to get paid for what I love doing well that just makes sense, does it not? For anyone wondering: yes there are a lot of trade-offs to working for yourself, and a major increase in self reliant responsibilities/ disciplines. You pick your hard, you pick your struggle: it's your life so ultimately it's all your own choice; where you want to go and where you'll end up.

3 years of making an income without a job

Before we dive into creating things as a job, or a way to make money, I need to tell you how I've sustained myself for 3 years creating without a job (i.e. working for myself).

This section is to give you some perspective on one path, but there are an infinite number of paths you could take or *create* to get to living **your** most preferred life. Do not think there are any less than an infinite number of paths you may choose for your life. 99% of the paths available are currently hidden from you. You can uncover them by any means of experiencing and creating things... To expand your imagination is to expand your available paths.

First off, when I dropped out of college I had already been working on the side to grow my income from a YouTube channel. This YouTube channel was literally just me documenting my journey to making money on the internet. Every day for my final semester: I woke up two hours before class at 5 AM and recorded a YouTube video. Then I would go and work on building my T-Shirt business by making designs and doing market research for two hours every day. This made me about $10,000 over the course of a year. Still three years later I get about $50/ month from this endeavor "passively". I worked for far less than minimum wage on this, that's usually how it goes at the start of making your own income. Although If you get it right you can build insane amounts of leverage.

As you can see.. It's a learning curve.. It did not all happen right away, it happened slowly. What comes next is even more so of a curve. I started another YouTube channel. This channel was on crypto currencies; something I was very passionate about at the time. This YouTube channel's first few videos took off by me being in the right time, right place and in its first three months made me the same $10,000 that my first channel and business took a year to make.

I then continued to make YouTube videos for this new channel and left my old one in the dust. After two years of the crypto channel I had made myself $400,000 and lost about $350,000 of it due to taxes and the general crypto price decline. So in reality, I made about $50,000 in 2 years from this endeavor. I also however made another $20,000 from doing freelance work, which I had no idea was possible: using my video and speaking skills as a service for others! My creation skills!

Now as I write this book I have abandoned most of these creative endeavors and my income is near $0, if I were to keep at my prior ventures they both would produce a sustainable income, however the point of my goal was finding work I want to do for the rest of my life. I enjoyed my endeavors prior, they were great and they helped me build valuable skills: but I feel as if where I am now I have finally found the work I want to do for the rest of my life, and that work is to write, learn, build and document. To ultimately write and build cool stuff others can find value in.

The story above skips a lot of details, but the point I'm trying to draw out is that there are an infinite number of ways to make money creating things, and with this infinite number of ways comes a barrage of choices when one is thinking about mixing creative output with economic output. The barrage is a good one though, you have so many options for crafting your ideal lifestyle that it's extremely exciting all while being overly terrifying.

The reason this barrage is good is because it makes someone who wants to create something for themselves flexible in the ways they can do it. For instance: I have been living off of savings while writing this book, but I have come to see a new path for myself on creating the life I want and that now involves doing freelance work and writing. Originally I can see myself playing the game of writing newsletters, books and building applications to help people as a lifelong game. Eventually I will end up winning this game but these worthwhile things take time, as all good things do.

The new approach to being a paid creator of things is really just to stay in the game as long as possible. The idea of freelance writing is pretty awesome too. I can build up my writing skill for life while making money on the internet. This takes a lot of pressure off of me playing my game at a sped-up pace and ultimately helps me stay in the game for longer, for forever (just keep swimming).

I only found this path because I have tried many ways of creating an income before on my own merit. Really it all boiled down to experimenting, and experimenting really is just your curiosity taking some good old-fashioned *action*.

That's my little story about creating for money, it doesn't have to apply to you, but I thought it may be useful for those who want to do more work in line with their creative abilities.

Reminder...No matter what you choose to do to earn money, you were built to create cool s**t. What you have to offer the world is unique to you and only you.

Finally for this section I'd like to mention that every paid occupation is a means of trading your creation value for money. You are paid by the amount of value you create in the economy, and if you add more value to the economy then you will get paid more.

Upping your value in the economy

Building skills is how you thrive, if you want to make money from your creative endeavors then your creative endeavors need to shed off value to people. This is done through learning skills or specific knowledge (specific knowledge is usually learned through acquiring a mix of unique skills).

Rather than explain to you how building skills is how you up your value, I'll just give you some simple examples. Let's look at 'value delivered' (with skill) vs 'value appraised'.

One thing I did a good amount in the last 2 years is freelancing. In my freelancing I started out by making free videos for a product I really liked. To make these videos I used my editing, design, and recording skills all mixed together. My free work served as my basis for getting people interested in my service. I landed my first clients by simply making noise (showing my work) and my starting rate was $200 per video. These videos usually took me less than 2 hours to make so right out of the gate I was pretty happy about it. But now, why did I get paid so much for so little time? Well because If the person hiring me were to do it themselves, doing all of what I offered, well it would take them a year or more to learn these skills (probably a lot more), and to mix them together? To know how to frame a video for YouTube, to make a thumbnail, to record and talk in a professionally presented manner, to edit it all together to pan, crop, zoom, add in effects to text, sound effects, all of these things: they take bits of specific knowledge to blend together. On top of these things my videos were in a very specific niche that required a deep understanding to make the video effective (more specific knowledge = higher pay).

So my service was valuable, and it got paid as such. I eventually upped my rate to $500/ video and made ~20 videos at this price point. Shortly after I stopped doing this service as It wasn't my main focus for playing my game, but it's still a set of skills I have and can use, one which I use bits of everyday now to make my own videos. This showed me my "silly little YouTube channels" gave me a ton of experience that most people just didn't have. What seemed like a monumental task to everyone else I just thought of as a somewhat easy one. Because after making thousands of recordings and videos, you get used to it, you get better at it, you can do it faster, you build skills!

I'm not trying to act all super macho with my example, because I'll tell you this: I don't do this work anymore because of the large effort it takes to get new clients (I'm lazy in this sense), as I write this I'm thinking about building some sort of system to tackle this for myself, but I'm still on the fence about it, I'm definitely curious. I wouldn't choose to do it as my life's work, but if it can fuel me to where I want to go, to playing my lifelong game (writing and reading a lot, making some cool useful s**t) then that's a wonderful thing.

Speaking of being curious... These skills came from exactly that: my curiosity. I was a curious human at McDonalds working away when I thought to myself "Can I make money on the internet?", "Yes.", "How?"... Then I started taking action on the first idea that caught my eye, and it led me here. I gained a bunch of different skills and I'm still trying to gain more. This is also why I'm writing this book, to improve my ability to write! I'm playing my game, it's fun to play.

I have a bunch more possible examples I could give here, but I'm going to take my lazier approach and let you do the work to figure some things out for yourself. I'll save you the wall of text by letting you think about: What are some skills you currently have that may be considered valuable?

We all have them, you have many, now: how can you hone them? What skills are worth building further? Are you already naturally building said skills? What do you need to learn to add value? What are you interested in that could mix with your existing skill sets in a unique way?

All of these questions are interesting ones to ask and see what your answers are. You don't have to answer all of them, or any of them, but if something sparks inside you when you ask any of these questions, follow that spark. Questions that lead to more questions are a good sign that you've found something you're sufficiently curious about. Something that will be easier to pick up or learn because you want to know the answers.

At the end of the day though, your skills determine your value to the economy and for better or worse: the value you bring is heavily correlated with the money you earn. This can be counteracted with underpaid workers who produce value well beyond other workers being paid the same amount. The key here is being a worker for someone else, this doesn't really happen the same if you work for yourself. One.) because there is no one else to compare your value to, and Two.) because you reap all the rewards that do or don't come based on the value you create.

If any of this chapter seems off to you, it may be. After all: I'm only 23, I still have a million things to learn... I don't think the amount of gaps I have will ever be filled, for me nor anyone. That is to say: *I only know that I don't know what I don't know.* This is a wonderful realization, that learning in life will never be over. There is always more to be uncovered, to be discovered. There is always more to learn.

On making money... and uhhh, other stuff.

To close off this chapter I'd like to tell you how many people will not fit into this mold of being a paid creator of things (Which is a good thing!).

I know that not everyone wants the same things, not everyone has the same interests, and not everyone needs (or wants) to work for themselves.

This is because everyone is completely unique. There is no person who is the same as another person in all ways, it just can't be so.

Each human is extremely different. Even identical twins with the same upbringing end up on completely different paths.

I mention this because I'm not trying to sell you a dream about working for yourself or being a creator of things on the internet. I know you can create amazing things, but there is an infinite number of ways in which you can do that. I don't want you to think that my path is also your path, because it's certainly not.

The best advice I think I would give to myself is to remain curious, follow that curiosity, and find little ways to do the things today that you would be doing in your most ideal version of life too. By living the life you want to live now in little ways, soon enough you may have the life you want. *'May'* because yeah, you still have to do the work to *create* it.

I don't put these final messages here to deter you from trying something like working for yourself, I only put it here to make you question why you are doing what you are doing, and if you then decide to go and try something bold: then so be it. That is, you finding your own way about the world, which is really all I want for everyone, to help them find their own way of existing. I feel like I have found mine more or less now especially writing this book, and it's made me much more capable of spreading love to those around me knowing I'm not torn about myself inside nearly as much as I used to be.

Finding yourself is really just figuring out what parts of you are your true reflections, and what parts are not actually you (deciphering projections of other people melted into your internal mirror). I know this chapter was supposed to be all about money, but money is not the golden light of our lives: **we** are. Our *selves*. And what we create is a large part of ourselves, so yeah, go create some stuff, okay?

Build those skills, make some money *maybe*, find your own way of existing. That was my gist about money which ultimately led to non-money thoughts. I'm going to leave this brain dump on the published pages now, if someone skipped over them that's fine too.

forty-two.

Finding your own approach

Creating many cool things and progressing in life is often really just about finding your unique path, not following a one-size-fits-all path.

You can blend other people's wisdom with your experiences to craft a personalized strategy to get what you want to see more of. Making (and taking) your own approach for life is a lot like having a custom house built to your dreams, desires and needs: you get to make it how you'd prefer, and the finished product is representative of that.

I had another 1500 words here but I didn't think they were worth reading, So instead I'll leave you the blank space on this page for you to "figure out your own approach".

forty-three.

Disregarding parts of your instincts

For all of my life I have been a big proponent for following your curiosity, and I still am. But I also want to make some clarifications about following curiosity in this chapter as I have discovered some unique aspects of instinctual patterns that I think are vital to one's success in pursuit of a better life of any sort.

What I wish to discuss in this chapter is a sense of awareness for one's thoughts, or rather: *consciousness*. Please keep in mind that I am still in my own process of trying to master my own mind and level of consciousness, so I am writing this chapter in a sort of selfish sense to help develop my own senses hoping it simultaneously triggers something in whoever is reading this.

Now, when should someone disregard their instincts? The short answer seems to be simple: Disregard your instincts when they don't serve your overarching external goals. The one who cannot control their basic desire for sex and food is more likely to be exploited on the path to where they want to be, and therefore will fail to reach where they are aiming to go in the first place. You and I both know the answers to many hard questions, but we do not know how to put the answers into practice. Mostly because with every question and answer comes another question.

How do we know when our instincts don't serve our overarching external goals? How do we figure out such goals? The simple answer is we must gain more consciousness! How do we gain more consciousness? Oh dear, now we are stepping in some worthwhile mud...

There are many practices that span over thousands of years trying to answer this question: yogi, Tao, Zen... and many more practices and/or religions of faith have been all put together to try and give the human mind more consciousness. Many have succeeded. Of the successes it has however always come down to the individual's commitment to the practices that help one gain a sense of control over their own mind. This takes a lifetime perhaps, many many years of invisible progress and invisible walls.

Isn't it perplexing? How can one simple question with a simple answer can be so extensively dug into? The fun part about this to me is that this whole sense of discovery outlines how we can throw aside our instincts at the right time. We have to reflect, and adjust! Simple right? But how do you do that? I think the answer is simple to this question too: we must try, and fail, and keep trying. At some point you will figure some parts out, maybe not all of it, but some. And that puzzle piece of your own consciousness may connect somewhere later on, who knows, how can we know? We can't, not yet.

This is the mind scramble I've had inside my head for some time now, sorry to lay it on you so abruptly.

Coming back to ditching your instincts, and following curiosity: You benefit a lot by using your instincts too, but your instincts cannot grow any better if you don't push outside of them to expand your consciousness. The same can be said for curiosity: if you deny yourself to be curious about something, you deny yourself to expand your limits on many fronts. Of course, this is all dependent on where you are as an individual in your search for what fulfills you, or what you are aiming to create.

In the end our results of where we will be tomorrow or at any point in the future is entirely based on what we do or think right in this very moment. Paying too much attention to where we are going is another way of denying ourselves from ever getting there. This is because if we focus only on the future we can easily forget what we need to do now to get there, to make it a reality. It also is not nearly as much fun to fantasize about the future more than you are enjoying the now of your existence, which is all you really ever have.

forty-four.

Thinking too much and creating nothing

If you think too much, you'll end up doing nothing and the only thing you will *create* is a buildup of tension in yourself. This is no good, and it's something I've been trying to tackle as I write this book.

In this chapter, I want to go over how someone may go about creating their own path and their own success, by adopting a more "one step at a time" approach vs the common "oh my goodness how am I going to do step 27 even though I'm still working on step 1!??!" approach.

What we put our attention on is indisputably going to cycle back to us in terms of what we are conscious of. If we are putting our attention on the lack of progress we have made, or the mountain still yet to be climbed, we will be constantly conscious of how far we have to go. What would be a more useful thing to focus our attention on? The step we are on, or the very next step: but no further than that. If we are paying attention to this we are conscious that we are making progress, and the loop of us making it up the mountain becomes inevitable.

This is a nice and simple way to look at climbing a mountain, but it also applies to nearly every human obstacle or dilemma. While writing this book I have caught myself thinking so much that I induced myself with major persistent headaches. My attention was scattered between making money, writing good stuff, and about four other "major" concerns in my life. The stress is common among people trying to solve multiple things in their life at once, but the most common symptom that I've found is a lack of doing, a lack of creating, and too much thinking 27 steps ahead.

When I really put my attention to one thing at a time, and take one step at a time, the headache of stress goes away, it fades to the background. The noise dissipates. When I am creating a pathway to walk on, things are much less stressful. Rather than drudging through the mud of my split attention, I'm just taking the first step and doing some things, creating the first push of momentum, the first bit of assurance that I can be on my way without overthinking every single day.

In the times that you think a lot, sometimes you can come up with good ideas. This is true, breakthroughs do happen and often stress can bring them about. Most of the time though, it's not just the thinking part that's doing the heavy lifting, it's where your thoughts are going, what you're paying attention to. The cycle of thoughts you have every day is put in frame by your attention. What are your current goals that you are paying attention to? What current problems are you facing? Your attention determines what your thoughts are thinking about, and what your brain sorts through on a daily basis.

If someone can't stop thinking about how they have no money. Their attention is all on this, a lack of money. They may be so overwhelmed at the prospect of getting a job and the twenty-one steps they have to go through that instead of getting up to fix their resume they choose to stay in bed all day. They can't take step one because they are scared about step twenty-one, they are worried they will get a job they don't like much at all, or they will be doing something they don't want to do. But they cannot know yet, can they? And if they find themselves in a job they do not like, can they not change their own position from there? Or would it be better to sit in bed all day and never know? Without doing anything, how can you expect your situation to change? You can't really. At least not much for the better. The lottery of life certainly isn't going to pick you as a winner if you don't even have a ticket. So *get up, do some things, grab a ticket, climb aboard!*

Putting this into another example is my own experience of how one thing you seemingly do today can have such a lasting ripple effect. 2 years ago I was enjoying a tool that someone made, so I took up the responsibility myself of making video guides on how to use the tool. No one paid me, but I felt it would be helpful to others and I wanted people to use the application without too many headaches. A few months went by and I got an inquiry to help a business with their videos. They hired me for 20 videos and paid me a really healthy amount of money.

Sure, not all of my random creative endeavors have turned into some super useful skill I can sell as a service, but many have, and these things only blossom when I am not thinking about the next twenty-seven steps to come. Instead I'm only thinking about the next step I need to take, or the current step I'm taking. I get lost in doing what I'm doing and by creating things: I make enough noise that it dissipates the lingering worries I have in my head. Like Nike says *"just do it"*... it's so cliche, but it's cliche because of how **true** it is. Why else would people repeat these infamous three words all of the time?

In just doing it, I can continue climbing the mountain, without worrying about when or how or if I'll make it to the top. I can enjoy the moment, and that's all there really is, so being able to do so is me freeing myself from the entrapment or worrying too much. All there is this step, then the next step. You never know where the step after may go, you never really know how anything could change the course of your life... how could you know? You can't! It's exciting, isn't it? Now you can focus your attention on what you want, rather than what you don't. Create some things even if they suck, make some noise because you never know how the step you're on will lead you to another obscure adventure. A final reminder to all of this: embrace your curiosity on your journey, it's one of your best friends in taking the next step and in figuring out how to best take the step you're currently on.

// I've been taking some time to put my attention on how this book is not just about how we should create *things*, but also how we should *create* new ways of thinking for ourselves, new ways of framing our goals and our lives. Because creating anything in this world requires you to create the proper conditions in your mind first. This is also why I mention curiosity so much, because it reduces your chances of overthinking, and allows you to just create some stuff without getting lost about step twenty-seven. Your focus is on the current step, and this is always the most important one really.

To create a better environment in our minds to create things, we need to build up our reputation with ourselves, to know we can get things done, to know we are capable of growth: to know that not everything must be a part of some major goal. As we develop a reputation of doing things, it becomes inevitable that we do more things, and the doing compounds over time, we can take step one without much of a worry at all, because we know how these things go: one step at a time. The first step in creating such an environment is mounted by simply taking it: by doing the first thing you can do.

Now go write down your thoughts or something, create a short reflection for two minutes. Or go do the other things you've been overthinking about.

forty-five.

Curiosity as a benchmark for success

"Success in anything is just a byproduct of learning, and learning is a byproduct of curiosity. Ultimately, if you are curious about something, you will be successful at it, and the more curious you are about it, the more successful you will be at it." – Naval Ravikant

Curiously I am mostly just curious to write this chapter. For me if I am curious about writing something or exploring it deeper in any sense then there is a much better chance whatever I'm following will bear more plump fruits for my brain to quench itself on. As it so happens this process of me being curious often leads to me being more successful in writing a good chapter or passage than if curiosity is lacking.

Some days we may trick ourselves to learn because we don't feel like it at that time, or trick ourselves to do the work because we know we don't always feel like doing what necessarily needs to be done.

When you are genuinely just curious there is none of that "I will get this done, whether I feel like it or not!". There is only a desire to learn more, and when you are on a learning spiral you usually end up learning a lot of useful things because your attention is far less split. You are focused in a sense of not needing to redirect your attention to learning, because you can't take your mind off of the subject even if you wanted to.

When you're curious about something it is much easier to pay attention. For when something peaks your interests it only makes sense you are more interested. A lot of life seems to be at the crossroads of interest and disinterest, we often force ourselves to be interested in things we just aren't. I think a better, more successful approach to this is to approach everything with as much curiosity as you can.

Let's say you were at an art museum, and you really did not feel all that interested in any one piece, but you are really curious in your everyday life about playing the piano. I'm sure there are even more curious things you have in your head but let's just use the piano for our current example. Rather than staring blankly at each portrait you can make up a game with your curiosity. If you're curious about the piano then think about what type of tune may play in the background for each piece of art, what music does it generate? What octave best suits the art? For me games are my preference in states of being restless or bored. The moment I can make something into a game that uses my curiosity is the moment I can begin to get lost in the here and now, even if only for some small period of time.

The title of this chapter though is not "how to appease boredom using your curiosity" it's something else isn't it? We are supposed to be speaking about *success*!

Well sure, you can successfully appease boredom by learning how to bring your curiosity into the moment... but how does this increase our levels of success?

There is this fate about success as mentioned in the opening quote that is told as "you will only be as successful as you are curious" - this is a hard truth to look at, but it's also not absolute: of course you can become lucky, of course there are paths that require less work than others that yield more fruit, which path will you be on with your own curiosity? I have no clue. I have no clue about a lot of things. What I do have a clue about is that using your curiosity is incredibly useful anyhow. How your specific curiosity is useful to you, that I have no clue, I just know it to be useful, somehow.

As I've dove headfirst into writing this chapter I'm now coming to realize that my curiosity about what I had to add to the opening quote has really led to me adding very little of anything new. The words Naval has spoken are so concise and at the same time looped that each curious question about the statement can be answered with another look into the statement.

Something that I can also tell you is even though I have a good amount of creations under my belt, all of the more successful ones were absolutely filled with curiosity. "How can I do this? What happens if I do this? What is this thing about?"

My extended stamina for learning that came from being curious led me to see much further success than in anything else. So, this is a testament to say that Navals words of wisdom are incredibly wise and accurate, at least in my own experience. If you reflect back you may see the same for your successes too.

In many ways I am still confused on where I should go next, I am curious about how curiosity works but can't seem to break my curiosity to go too much further than that. I've asked many other people what they think about curiosity and if there's any wrong way to approach being curious. The most common response was a collection of: "No, I don't think there is any wrong way, I do not put limits on my curiosity I just let it do its thing."

It's an incredible feeling to be learning something not just because you have this large external goal to fulfill and need a piece of knowledge to get there, but rather learning because you just *must* know more, you are genuinely interested in what the world holds and you need to know. This type of learning that is purely driven through genuine curiosity is what has driven all of my biggest successes in life thus far (as far as I can tell).

Before we end this chapter I'll let you sit with the quote here again...

"Success in anything is just a byproduct of learning, and learning is a byproduct of curiosity. Ultimately, if you are curious about something, you will be successful at it, and the more curious you are about it, the more successful you will be at it." – Naval Ravikant

forty-six.

Agency: figure it out, yourself!

This chapter is not about "agencies". Speaking of this though... is it not odd that the term "agency" is basically a group of collected people doing stuff, but the trait of having "agency" in one's own life is really about thinking for one's self? this is weird, right? Anyways... let's talk about the latter form of agency.

There were these words I read the other day, they made me realize how different people have different levels of agency, and this shows itself in interesting ways. For example...

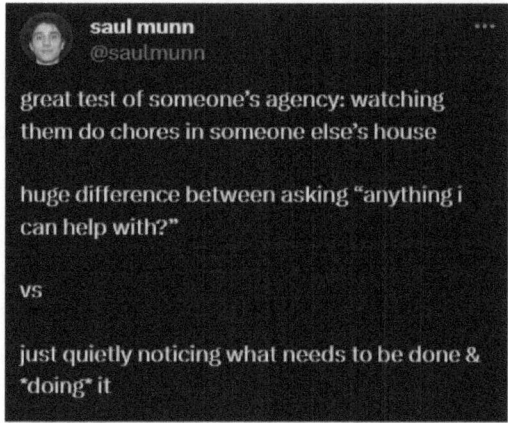

Someone who has a high level of agency will take it upon themselves to figure things out, as opposed to jumping at the first moment of their own doubt, they are more prone to let it sit for a second to see if they can or cannot figure it out on their own. Having more agency can be very useful in creative endeavors too as it lets your curiosity crawl around a lot more, as you are using your own head a lot more as opposed to someone else's.

The main reason I am talking about agency in this book of creation and how to create things is because I think it fills a gap. And that gap is the part of consciousness, or rather: awareness.

To be at a high level of agency also means one must be aware of their surroundings and how they mold into them. Someone with a higher level of awareness would recognize that asking if there's "anything they can help with" may just put more strain on someone who is already clearly overwhelmed. Of course, this example is not always suitable, sometimes you do have to genuinely ask questions. Questions are great for learning, and the best form of learning is found in exploring one's curiosity.

There are a multitude of other things we could talk about in the example I've shown: some people may not be used to cleaning, doing chores, some people may not have the same set of standards for one's household, etc. etc. The important part of the example is that in many ways it still holds true!

If you want to see how much agency someone has, give them vague instructions and see how long it takes them to come asking you questions. I'm sure there have been many times where you have gone to ask someone a question but they could not or did not answer, so what did you do? You figured it out on your own. This has happened to me in many cases when someone texts me to help them with a problem, they are having that is technology related. Oftentimes I don't see a message for help for an hour, and by the time I get to it the person has already solved their own problem.

Sure, asking for help is useful at speeding up your current problem, but this brings in two other burdens at the same time. The first one being the burden you put onto someone else to use their time to help you. The second burden is that they can do your homework for you in the sense that you'll have the solution, but you won't have learned much at all, and if this is a recurring problem it would be much better for you to figure out how to solve it for yourself now. Even if the problem is not apparently recurring, you'd be surprised how learning one process can transfer to many other processes (everything is connected).

This idea of solving things yourself; using your own agency, is incredibly useful in a few other realms of life, but the two I'm concerned with right now are curiosity, and creation.

First, let's talk about curiosity and its mix with agency. If you are someone who is curious about something the main thing you will tend to do is ask questions. This is how you learn anything really, you ask questions and you find answers. In terms of agency, being curious is largely trying to figure out what comes next, by yourself. You cannot ask anyone else but yourself what you should be curious about, or where to go next in your curiosity. The only person who has these answers is you, and the only way you'll find them is if you become a dedicated agent of your own curiosity.

Think of it like this: you're on a secret spy mission, akin to Tom Cruise in Mission Impossible. Your objective? Tracking down your curiosity. This pursuit to me would be the ideal plot of your life's movie. But how does one excel as an effective agent of curiosity?

Well you have to be aware. You have to be aware of what you're doing and if it's inline with your curiosity or if it's more a part of the conditioning you've become subject to throughout your life by the environment around you. This is not to say that doing anything that you are not curious about is a waste of time, or a bad thing, most of life is not framed in pure curiosity. This is more to say that if you want to be curious you have to make yourself aware of the things you naturally gravitate towards and then be a dedicated enough agent to follow such things.

Now, if we are to examine the use of agency in creating things it can be applied in a bunch of ways. Teaching things to yourself, overcoming obstacles in your work, figuring out how you may go about approaching *just getting started*. The act of creation invariably presents a myriad of questions and possible answers.

Using agency when it comes to the bombardment of assorted questions and answers is really just realizing that you will not know until you try, and that the majority of your analysis is only inducing further paralysis. Again, agency is mostly just a mix of your ability to be aware of where you fit into your surroundings and how conscious you are about what you are/ aren't doing and how it is working or not working. When we bring more agency into creating things it helps us move more boldly to get the results we are after in our craft.

Think for yourself. By thinking for yourself you are constantly training yourself and learning more about yourself. And to know yourself deeper, to know more in general about the world, this is an incredibly useful skill when it comes to traversing all of life, including creation and curiosity. // *good luck agent, on your super cool mission.*

forty-seven.

Creating your own home

On the internet, or in your own brain, or maybe in real life.

A house is not a home when you first move into it. Similar to buying something used, it is not felt to be yours until some time after. This is because a home consists of small bits of your soul. A home is a place or environment you can reliably feel at peace in. A home is a place, person, or thing that keeps your mind contained amidst all the jumble.

It's my belief that there are three types of houses in your life that you can create into homes. You don't have to turn all of these housings into homes, but you can. As always, you have a choice! And isn't it more fun when we have a choice?

The three types of housing I'm talking about are as follows:

First, **Your mind.**

This is the house of your own self, your thoughts, your consciousness. This is where dreams come to be and come to pass. It's where all of your memories are held. Your mind is the house that must be turned into a home in order to let yourself prosper. This transformation can really only be done so with the same magic ingredient that turns any type of house into a home. The secret ingredient? Love. To love yourself is to nurture in your mind what you want to see more of, to take steps not in a panicky or an anxious way, but to accept each step as a move deeper inside your mental housing. To be able to realize that each struggle is also growth: this is realized with less resistance when you put love into the equation.

Being able to step outside of your own self critic, and see the flowers of your mind blooming. This is how the house of your mind can slowly, over a lifetime, be turned into a home... You may have a different approach to this, that's fine too. The main message I only wish to put on display here is that a house must be transformed into a home, it does not come pre fitted as such. You must put in the currency of not only money, but energy, to get your desired output.

Second, **Physical housing**.

Where you live in the physical realm. This is referring to not only your shelter or literal house, but also the people and things that surround you. In the physical realm there are many ways to make a house into a home. The most important things to consider when turning your physical realm from a house to a home are *where you live*, *who you're with* and *what you're doing*. Notably, these decisions seem to be largely the three most important for all types of homes.

In order to turn your house into a home the steps are really the same here as the ones for the mind. Time plus effort (energy inputted) = your home. Struggle is a natural part of growth, and therefore to grow into a quaint home you will likely encounter a fair bit of struggle. This is not me trying to be wise, I am only trying to serve as an active reminder in your head so you don't quit before the growth shows... not that it will always come right away, or at all in the way you expect it to.

Third, **Digital housing.**

This is about your slice of pie on the web, your local website, and/or your digital environment. Now that I'm writing how to turn a third type of housing into a home I'm seeing that it's all really the same. If you want to turn your Digital realm to your digital home then you'll need to act with intention, encounter some headaches (struggle) and grow through it all with love (and faith in yourself for what lies ahead). Same as the last house to home processes. A digital home however is a much less wandered area in typical research and texts as it's been around for a short time in comparison.

The idea of having your own digital environment only really felt like a real concern even to me over the last few years. In relation to your decision on "what you're doing" in life, your digital housing matters a whole lot. As I mentioned in the Consumption Decay chapter of this book, if you set your digital environment up to have you consuming all day long, you won't get much joy nor fulfillment from what you're doing, and that can leave you depleted of a ton of important things for life. If we are to consider other parts of creating a digital home we need to mainly pay attention to how the configuration of our digital realm prospers towards what we want to see more of (and makes us do the work that matters). If our digital environment is not pushing us to where we want to go or to what we want to see, then we must continue to craft it and curate it. Like the transformation of your mind's house to a home, this is a long and ongoing process.

For all types of homes: Once you make your house into a home you still must maintain it with reasonable effort to keep it this way. Such is the nature of having nice things; they require sustained effort.

Making a home is not an entirely dreadful struggle though, rather it is first and foremost: a wonderful adventure... you just have to figure out how you can see it in the second lens more than the first. As I may have mentioned before, a useful ingredient for doing such is love.

The human who cannot love is not strong, they are broken, they are the ones who need love the most, even if they run from exactly what they need at every turn. A home is made with love. Your family recipes' secret ingredient? Love. Your optimism for a brighter future is crafted with? Love.

So to repeat myself again: In order to make any housing into a home I think there is always an element of tenderness involved: a dash, a sprinkle, or multiple handfuls... of *love*.

For the mind this is aided by loving oneself. For the physical realm this is aided by being surrounded by people you love. For the digital realm this is aided by the love to craft and curate a welcoming environment for yourself.

// Each acquired home makes the next house homier.

forty-eight.

The undercover creation agent

A 23-year-old's approach to a joyous//more full life. I'm going to try and make this not all about myself, but as I mentioned in the beginning of this book: this is more so about me showing you possible paths to your life than it is me telling you which one to take, or to take any one path at all.

Ultimately, I want you to create your own path using things you find useful from this book, or things you find yourself cringing about. Create a path you don't want to be on and start a new path with this found basis. Either way: here's a part of a new path I'm trying on that I think is something many would frame in a sense of "Wage slavery", or "Death of identity" if they were me, or if the me today was the same me from two years ago. This is also my way of coping with the grim reaper inside of me and shining more light to the joyous reaper.

First off, creation. Creation is an important part of life, to create things to me is one of the absolute major points of life, I've already given the speal on why I think this a few times but for quick refresh: Non-zero-sum creation = new stuff, more stuff, uniquely made stuff to each individual that walks this earth = more cool stuff = endless cycle of human progression and evolution. I am on this secret mission with the objective of creating new world views for myself that I can utilize in my own creations to make them more impactful and truthful.

For the last three years since I dropped out of college, I made an internal oath to myself that I would do all of the things in my power not to "work a job". It became part of my identity, that I had this entire entrepreneurial spirit inside myself figured out. Well, after three years I've certainly made some large ground, I've made more than I would have made working almost any job, and subsequently lost more money too than I would have otherwise. But the thing is, I've spotted a new branch to swing from, and this branch is non entrepreneurial in nature, it's more so a branch of having a job.

This metaphorical branch is me seeing that my lack of an income since I left my main business to the side has a dire effect on my entrepreneurial spirit. Losing money each month rather than gaining will do that to a person. It's disheartening, for sure, a lot of typical business progress and progress by everyone around you is based on "How much money did you make this month?", as opposed to "What new things have you learned?" or "Are you any more excited about life this month than the last?" *(yes!)*.

This is how I've come to see that having an income means a lot for the longevity of my entrepreneurial spirit. Although my identity may say "You said you would never work a job!! Not after McDonalds!" I countered it to "We can work a job or earn money in a way that pushes us forward on our own business, we can develop our skills while making an income, we can do it all while building the business, we can collect secret inside info to help us excel in our lifelong path" ...

It stumped me for some time, but upon reading more into being in a "flow state" via "Flow" by Mihaly Csikszentmihalyi I came to the conclusion that I don't need to always be on this absolute path of working for myself or being my own boss. I realized I can find great joy in being lost in just about any activity that meets the criteria of being in a flow state, and this is especially so with my background motivation for doing something being in line with my perceived life's work.

The three main criteria for being in a flow state:

- **Challenge-Skill Balance:** Task difficulty matches skill level.
- **Clear Goals and Feedback:** Know what to achieve and how well you're doing.
- **Autotelic Experience:** Enjoyment derived from the activity itself.

I can turn a job into this state especially if it's inline with my ulterior motives in writing or creating cool things. (writing, graphic design, web design, and other growing related interests/skills/curiosities)

I can be an undercover agent in an involved state of a job and still enjoy my existence. I can learn more things about different parts of the world and quench my curiosity about the intricacies of a system I haven't been involved with first hand. I can be an undercover worker gathering data for my own ventures. This is the fun framing I have made for myself to help me enjoy/succeed this mission.

I could have framed it all as this: "I have to work a job that I won't love just to talk to people I don't necessarily have the same interests with so I can progress? And I'll have to change my freedom level? Oh so grim, I hate this new path of life" – See, the same thing, put differently, is far less fun. When I have made something into a mission of sorts, with a plan of improving my progress to get to where I want, it's a lot more fun. One can become lost in such a game, in a good way, in a joyous way.

I also want to mention as a part of this chapter that this book is by no means my complete work, noting that I still have yet to take on this undercover mission for a longer period of time, I still must see where it takes me, and come back once again to report to my commanding officer: which is you, the reader of my creations and writings, the person whom I would not exist without. I may exist, but to be heard is a different form of existing, it's a non lonely way of existing. This way is much more fun: it's much better framing.

This book is a collection of thoughts on my missions I have put together, so I figured I might as well spill the beans on this new mission I just constructed as I'm writing this book. It's abstract as most of life's problems and matching solutions are.

It's far from being as simple as the best move on a chess board, because life's large dilemmas cannot be so easy, for that would take away all the fun and ongoing curiosity we often frolic in, wouldn't it?

// Note, Six weeks after writing this chapter: I have more context now, things to add! It doesn't take much to gain some more important context.

I went and asked my mom and best friend what they admired/respected about me (I highly recommend you do this too!) and they both mentioned how they admire me for being able to take the massive risk of working for myself and respected my aim for things other than money on my priorities list. They also mentioned that they respected my own self responsibility.

The reason I'm telling you this is because it added a lot of contexts to my mission. I realized that I have a lot more hope than I had previously for myself. My blind spots have been reduced and I can see there are more pathways available to me than just "job" vs "work for myself". Now in each path I can move forward with more confidence in my own abilities. No matter what, I will make it enjoyable, I have made up my mind, and I will frame it as such.

forty-nine.

Waves of joy in all the crevasses

"The waiting rooms of psychiatrists are filled with rich and successful patients who, in their forties or fifties, suddenly wake up to the fact that a plush suburban home, expensive cars, and even an Ivy League education are not enough to bring peace of mind. Yet people keep hoping that changing the external conditions of their lives will provide a solution. If only they could earn more money, be in better physical shape, or have a more understanding partner, they would really have it made. Even though we recognize that material success may not bring happiness, we engage in an endless struggle to reach external goals, expecting that they will improve life." – Mihaly Csikszentmihalyi

I think a large part of humanity has become more aware that more things do not equal more happiness. The quote above was written 1990 in the book "Flow"; over 30 years ago from when I write this chapter now. Not much has changed in the structure of how humans think about reaching happiness in life, but so much has changed in every other metric. Why is that? What's going on?

To get a deeper look at these questions, this chapter is going to use some of my limited experience in life and also call from the book in which I got the opening quote from.

Why are humans still hell bent on external goals being the key to a better life? What's going on here?

Humans appear to be hell bent on external goals being the answer mostly because it's something that can't be proved against with concrete evidence until the feeling or realization is personally made. Humans think this is the key to improving their lives at first because they have limited other windows in their own frame for a happy healthy life. A new frame is opened when one realizes all those around them are chasing external goals to no end with the ideal of reaching a better life, yet they are never reaching it... endlessly reaching for the next big thing.

Another reason for the herd to chase external goals is because it has worked for some people, or at least it has *appeared* to work for some people. This is because many people can find a great deal of joy in a pursuit that others look at as drudgery. Any activity can seemingly be boring to the outside viewer and simultaneously invigorating to the active participant. Some people while in the pursuit of external goals (luckily) fall into a place of internal fulfillment. The number of people who end up falling into this place by accident is enough to make many others come after a similar path, but there is something not being seen here.

The achievement of the goals did not bring a better life, but rather what ended up being the improver of life was the actions comprising the pursuit. The activity one was able to find themselves enjoying, or lost in. An activity was the improver, not so much a result.

"*Most enjoyable activities are not natural; they demand an effort that initially one is reluctant to make.*" – Mihaly Csikszentmihalyi

This statement adds to this point that the pursuit of external goals is -by chance- bound to create some people who end up falling into doing an enjoyable activity. So, many people try to follow someone else's path and end up doing activities that they cannot detach their own self consciousness from, therefore they do not end up enjoying the activity at hand... they are too busy thinking about what fruit it will yield them or how it will make others see them. They are too worried and anxious about their own self to enjoy the activity.

And also as a note: external goals are not bad or good, they are just a tool that can be used for one's betterment or one's own demise in terms of actual improvement of life. The key with getting a desired result while using any tool is that you know how to use the tool correctly.

Now, spinning these threads I just framed in your head about enjoying an activity. I want to add some more thoughts in relation to creation and curiosity.

First, some relevant things...

My new viewpoint:
I often thought that to live a fulfilled and happy life you would need all this fancy stuff and a certain job or role that you are adamant about, but as it turns out the life of a king awaits you by getting lost in any activity that demands an adequate amount of skill and effort (skill is often built from a prerequisite of curiosity).

A dire loop of modern man:
"Many people feel that the time they spend at work is essentially wasted—they are alienated from it, and the psychic energy invested in the job does nothing to strengthen their self. For quite a few people free time is also wasted. Leisure provides a relaxing respite from work, but it generally consists of passively absorbing information, without using any skills or exploring new opportunities for action. As a result life passes in a sequence of boring and anxious experiences over which a person has little control." – Mihaly Csikszentmihalyi

The task of life:
"The task is to learn how to enjoy everyday life without diminishing other people's chances to enjoy theirs." – Mihaly Csikszentmihalyi

Now that I've put some more frames for reality out there for you to view your life with, I want to elaborate on the use of creation on curiosity in relation to the state of flow (finding yourself lost in an activity, which makes any activity a very enjoyable undertaking).

Curiosity is by large a great starting point for doing things, for getting up and seeing how an activity feels. For this reason I believe that curiosity is probably the best driver of anyone's path to find themselves lost in an activity, and ultimately to find themselves in a flow with the task at hand. As opposed to being lost in the clouds thinking about where they're going or what fruits they will be able to harvest in X amount of time.

Curiosity fills the role in many ways of leading a horse to water and making it drink. Although the saying goes "You can lead a horse to water, but you can't make it drink", curiosity is a great guide because it makes it hard not to drink the water, or rather: If someone is genuinely curious, they will try some stuff, they will do some things. This is the best place to start if you're trying to find activities that you can get lost in. Although in the book "Flow" Mihaly claims that you could get lost in virtually any activity, I think the best way to get lost at all is to begin by trying things that you are curious about. If you are curious about something you are more prone to challenge yourself, you are more prone to use and develop your skill and therefore you are more prone to enjoy what you're doing.

Creation falls into this puzzle by the means of craft. Anytime you are involved in an activity that puts you in a flow like state where time is no longer, this is also a time where you are always found creating something worthwhile. Perhaps you are creating something tangible, or perhaps you are creating something more spiritual. Nonetheless: you are in a craft like trance, and the result you created is a better life. Not through acquisition of things of the accomplishment of external goals, but by the means of internal fulfillment, and the creation of more peace of mind inside yourself.

// this is how I see it at least, maybe you think I'm full of woo woo, don't worry: sometimes I think the same of myself too... but all the woo woo adds up in some odd but good ways, so I let the woo woo take a seat, I let it hang around, I let it help me get into flow, and then I let it go. It always comes back though.

fifty.

Letting people convince you that something is wrong with you

In 2013 when I was 13, I was using photoshop and a 4D text modeler to create specialized YouTube backgrounds for people. And I loved all of it, learning how to create new effects, putting my brain juices towards making something unique, something new, something impressive, something each person would love. I ended up learning a ton in a short amount of time while having an absolute blast because I was effortlessly diving into my curiosity and my own true nature.

Guess what though? I never pursued it much further after I turned 14 because it "wasn't a high earning career path" to be in graphic design. When I was 14 I didn't know any better, that my parents were just humans like me and they weren't some omnipotent beings that knew everything about everything. I love my parents, they are the best. But of course now I can see how being highly skilled in graphic design is not a low paying job when using the internet. I know of many paths to make more than enough money using this skill... but this isn't the point I'm trying to make.

What I'm trying to say is this: it makes me sad when I see others bashing on someone genuinely interested in doing something. Most people do not understand that we are in the age of the internet: anyone who is curious enough about something can excel in many ways, money included! Encouragement is scarce.

Nowadays I see many graphic designers around who have been going for 10+ years and have an incredible body of work as well as a high demand for their work. It's all so common, I even forgot about this lost dream of mine. With the tide it went along with many of my other aspirations that my younger self didn't see as a high enough earning potential. When I was 14 my curiosity already started being guided by my future thoughts of the earning of money, how ridiculous this is, how sad.

I know better now, and there is so much to be learned, it's actually pretty awesome where we find ourselves today regardless of the past. Skills you hone do matter, and on the internet the person with a high level of skill across one or many domains has so much leverage: no matter if they can earn a high salary via a job, there is so much potential in so many avenues.

The best way to develop skill is to learn, and the best way to learn is to be extremely curious. This means that yes, once again, curiosity is our guiding light, and as a kid it can be easy to have this light covered up, so I'm telling you to let it lead more of your way, it's a wonder; being curious, and it's another wonder to follow that curiosity.

I still remember how I had a blast when I was 13, made speed art videos of my process, and designed cool stuff because it was fun, I learned without trying, *it was that interesting* to me at the time. I was so curious about each part of what I could create, how I could improve, what new techniques I had yet to know. But the little old me got his dreams crushed when he turned 14, with a new thought of having to go do something with a higher earning potential.

This brings me back to a quote from the last chapter: *"The task is to learn how to enjoy everyday life without diminishing other people's chances to enjoy theirs."* – Mihaly Csikszentmihalyi

I think this is a large part of adulting's faults. They don't know how much they don't know, so they toss you around in their own perception of joy/ "what is best" (which is really often times *your* future misery you just don't know any better as a child to go against the grains put onto you. Or if you haven't figured such a thing out yet in your early adult years, that you know you best, and that your parents are only human, you can end up thinking something is wrong with you when it is often not. I'm not saying that you're perfect, but rather that the curious parts of you that you think to be odd or wrong are often your biggest strengths.

An example: Someone may make you feel like there is something wrong with you because you don't enjoy leisure time or a vacation with ample idle time... you would rather find yourself working on your latest project, or learn more about what you're curious about, or go for a run. This is sort of me, I am restless on vacation, I can't sit on the beach for long before I have the desire to go work on a project of mine, write an essay, design my website further, or in general just do something that puts me in a flow like state: do something I'm curious about doing.

To supplement this I read a lot on vacation, but I just can't seem to sit and do nothing for a week, one day or two days sure, 30 minutes maybe an hour alone with my thoughts is nice, but after a certain point I lose the enjoyment aspect of vacation. You may be thinking about my ideals and be dreaming about just bathing in the sun, and that's just how it is. We are all different in nature. If you want to increase how you mend with others, it's important to know there's nothing wrong with you. This way you can find how you operate, and best mesh with other's preferences.

We all have different needs, and many people have their optimal experience under different conditions. Someone may very much enjoy skipping rope, another person may think this activity is the absolute worst. Nothing is wrong with either of these people, they are just different humans with different preferences. We all inherently know this, but we seemingly can't apply it to all senses of life. We forget that not everyone is thinking about what we individually enjoy in contrast with their own preferences.

In general, the quest for life still comes back to the quote I mentioned earlier. To follow your curiosity without breaking someone else's chance of exploration.

"The task is to learn how to enjoy everyday life without diminishing other people's chances to enjoy theirs." – Mihaly Csikszentmihalyi

Here it is so you don't have to go looking back again. This quote puts this chapter perfectly into place. To help you avoid being knocked off your own path, and so you can encourage others to keep going on theirs too.

fifty-one.

Making the internet a better place

Here are five "secrets" that are really just reminders for a more humane interweb, do indulge, if you will.

The internet is a big place. A place where it's dark at night and can be even darker during the day: but it doesn't have to be this way, you can shine some light for yourself, and for others. Today I'm here to share with you five secrets to thriving in the sinister realm of the internet because the world could use a little more friendly light, couldn't it?

Secret #1: Harnessing encouragement

Use your encouragement powers. The internet is a wonderful place for encouragement: if you see someone doing something and you relate, or it helps you, tell them! why not? You make friends, people feel good about the cool things they are doing/creating, and the world is a better place for you encouraging such.

It's wild, we have this immense amount of impact on those around us by simply telling them how much good they have done for us. Most people take it for granted, but you can quite literally change someone's entire month for the better by simply expressing how they've helped you.

Example from my experience:

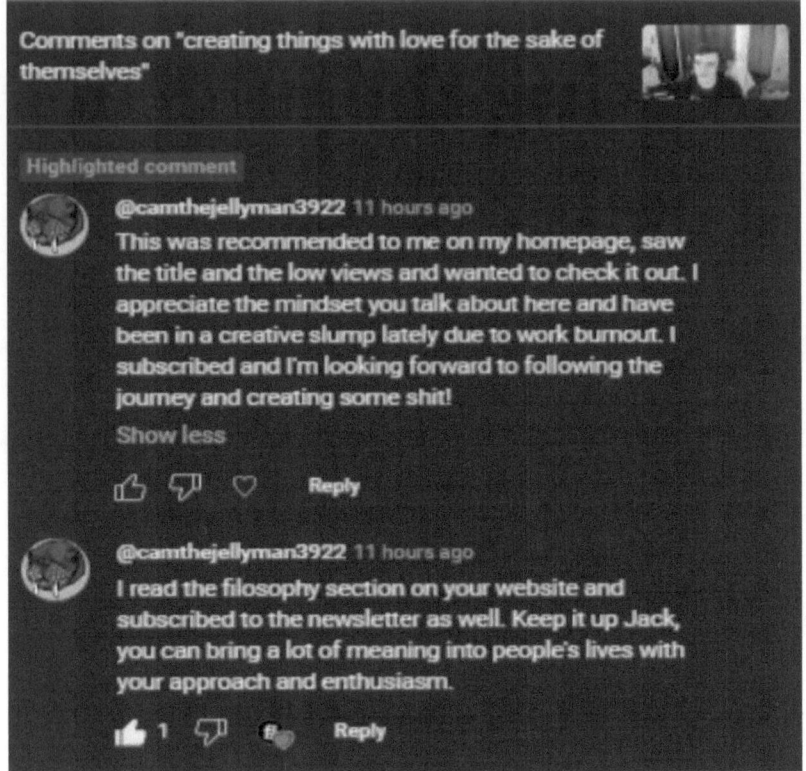

It's these types of comments that someone doesn't HAVE to type at all, but they do: and it can change someone's entire life direction. thank you camthejellyman, you're a legend, I'm tearing up now.

Secret #2: Refrain from being a weeniehead.

Perhaps you have forgotten, but there is an immense amount of options for how you can choose to act on the internet. A lot of these options involve acting like a curious friend, a supportive stranger, a respectful conversationalist, etc. You could also choose to be a weeniehead. If you want to make your experience more fun, however, I will tell you a secret: You won't enrich anyone's experience, including your own, by being a weenie head.

Again, to repeat: the second secret to thriving on the internet is simple but often forgotten: **refrain from being a weenie head.**

Secret #3: Be more genuinely curious.

On the internet it is often about right and wrong, funny and unfunny, cool or not cool: but this is just no fun for a lot of participants. You have to put somebody down or discourage one person to encourage another. A much more fun approach to converse and participate in the internet is to just be genuinely curious.

What do you want to know? What interests you? What questions have yet to be asked? — Stuff like this (approach with less ego, more curiosity). If you don't have anything to say, then ask what you do not know but wish to know. By doing this you become a lot more earnest and the internet becomes less dark and more fun, there is so much to know, and it's all reachable if you're ready to ask questions.

Being genuinely curious is fun, and it's a great precursor to a lot of great things. Very useful on the internet, and in all of life.

Secret #5: Make friends, not followers or leaders.

Followers on the internet are not nearly as valuable as having friends. Sure followers will read your stuff, watch your things, and converse with you sometimes. But it's a shallow relationship by nature: you cannot be friends with everyone, but you can follow them all (this is fine!).

If you've taken secrets #2 and #3 to heart then this shouldn't be too hard, matter of fact it will likely come naturally as you explore for yourself curiously. People who develop their own sense of self find it easiest to find others because they can easily know what environments they will enjoy being in.

"Don't walk behind me; I may not lead. Don't walk in front of me; I may not follow. Just walk beside me and be my friend." — Albert Camus

Secret #5: Focus on what you want to see more of

This secret has been brought to my attention by Visakan Veerasamy (@visakan). It's really simple, if you want to see more of something, then focus on it!

If you want the internet to bring your life more joy, then your focus should be on how you can do that. If you want the internet to bring your life less anger then focus on how it can bring you more joy (don't focus on the anger, you don't want to see more of it!).

Create the change you want to see. Maybe you want to develop more friendly people in your internet bubble, then focus on being a friend worth having! Be a proponent of your own mission, and focus on what you want to see more of.

// Encouragement, kindness, and friendliness go a longer way than most think. Especially on the internet where one may find themselves in darkness even on the brightest days.

fifty-two.

Creating the conclusion

The final countdown! This chapter is likely the final chapter for this book. I know it's weird for me to announce it, but I feel a need to put this creation into the world and I don't want to let it sit in the dark corner by itself for too long.

This chapter is a reflection of my own thoughts and may inspire you to create some cool shit. You don't have to read it, but you didn't have to read any of this book either. Keep in mind that this book is largely skimmable, so you can open any chapter and get a separate (hopefully useful) message.

I waited a lot of my life to write a book, I always thought writing a book was reserved for a special and select few "writer people"… but this is far from the truth: writing a book has always just been reserved by those who write books. If you don't write a book then you'll never have written a book, y'know? Seems pretty obvious writing this now.

If you don't create something then how can you hope to have created something? You cannot, of course. This is kind of my final message to you with a clear example: You must create what you want to create, you must create what you want to see in your own hands, and you cannot dwell forever about the invisible blockades in your way. Because not only are they invisible, but most of them never existed anywhere but in your head the entire time. Let your curiosity guide you when in doubt, everything will be okay in the end, if it is not okay then it is not yet the end.

That's the gist of this book, I wrote it selfishly hoping I could get my own thoughts onto paper to be understood in my mission on this floating rock. In the selfishly curious writing of this book I have found so much more than I originally thought would come from writing it. I have found a higher sense of optimism and love for my fellow human... I'm really not sure how this feeling transpired to be, for I didn't set out to love others or be optimistic for others, I really set out to understand my own brain through writing about my thoughts. In one way this book is a keepsake of words to me, a diary. In another way this book is a part of my soul's scrambled feelings put into text... some of which parts may make more sense than others.

If this book has transpired a sense of positive force in anyone, or gotten anyone to create something, then it has fulfilled my goal for putting it out there. Books are amazing things, this won't be my only book, but it is my first... so the fact that you are reading this right now means more than you think.

If you feel you have been impacted in any way by this book please feel free to DM me on twitter @jackfriks, or email me @ jack@frikit.net. I will be collecting all such messages to add them to my inspiration wall (a digital collection of nice things people have said to me) and replying to all of them too ☺

It's time now to put the creation of this book to print, well first I must edit it, that should only take a week or two (fingers crossed). *// It took much longer.*

// 1st edit on this chapter: past jack did not yet know that editing a book is much less fun than writing a book.

// 2nd edit on this chapter: editing is the slow roast part of making something that's beautiful (new framing)

// 3rd edit on this chapter: writing a book that's going to print is scary!! At the same time, it is also incredibly freeing. Once it's printed -and there's no going back- you can finally let go of the idea that it was ever going to be truly complete or finished. The real process in anything creative is a never ending one.

Thank you. For joining me on this journey of my own creation. I couldn't have done it without you: a fellow human and friend.

Now, you were built to create, so go create!

your friend,
jack ♠ ♥

Free resources

My newsletter, blog and hub
My newsletter is the birthplace of this entire book, had I never started writing over there this book might have never come to be. This newsletter is essentially a bi-weekly dive into mastering yourself, igniting your creativity, and quenching your curiosity, so you can live a better life (or at least that's my idea... I'm still figuring this life thing out too y'know) This is likely where I'll be posting my writing from my next book too.
Link: https://frikit.net/subscribe
Read more: https://frikit.net/blog

YouTube Documentation
While writing this book I started making daily updates on the book by talking about certain chapters and their points via video. If you want to see an authentic behind the scenes of a part of this book's writing, then checkout my YouTube.
Link: https://www.youtube.com/@frikitdotnet/

Curiosity Quench
Another thing you may find helpful in exploring your curiosities if you don't know where to start, or just want to get off of TikTok more, is an app I'm building called curiosity quench. It's a large work in progress, as we all are 😊.
Link: http://curiosityquench.com

X/Twitter

The main place I go to in terms of social media, I write many things here too and love meeting new curious friends on the internet here.
Link: https://twitter.com/jackfriks

No matter where you go, I encourage you to follow your curiosity and I encourage you to follow the dimly lit path you may be scared to walk currently. You have something to offer this world that no one else can: **your** creations. You can light the way for yourself and countless others. Yes, **you,** can.

$$(\check{} \cup \check{}) /$$

good luck, my friend ✧.°

Reading List

If you're looking for books to read, then here is a list of many books I have read and been recommended on my journey that I found useful and that may help you in your journey too.

I also want to make note that my way of reading books is not about finishing each book: but getting the useful parts out for my current situation and then acting on them, so some of these books I have not read to completion, but just read the parts I wanted to. You should read however you do best, but I thought I'd throw this out there because I think many people view reading as an arduous thing, when it shouldn't be most of the time.

Read however you are best interested. The end goal being enjoy the book you're reading, and you'll enjoy reading as a whole. Okay, here's the list...

"**INTROSPECT**" by Visakan Veerasamy

"**FRIENDLY AMBITIOUS NERD**" by Visakan Veerasamy

"**The Almanack of Naval Ravikant**" by Eric Jorgenson

"**Flow: The Psychology of Optimal Experience**" by Mihaly Csikszentmihalyi

"**Love Yourself Like Your Life Depends on It**" by Kamal Ravikant

"**Deep Work**" by Cal Newport

"**Atomic Habits**" by James Clear

"**The Pathless Path**" by Paul Millerd

"**Four Thousand Weeks**" by Oliver Burkeman

"**The Minimalist Entrepreneur**" by Sahil Lavingia

"**Steal Like an Artist**" by Austin Kleon

"**The Creative Act**" by Rick Rubin

"**The Rational Optimist**" by Matt Ridley

Most important thing to read: *whatever you're genuinely interested in.*

www.ingramcontent.com/pod-product-compliance
Lightning Source LLC
Chambersburg PA
CBHW031103080526
44587CB00011B/801